TREASURES OF THE NAVAJO

▼▼▼

Theda Bassman

TREASURES
of the
Navajo

by **THEDA BASSMAN**

photographs by **GENE BALZER**

NORTHLAND PUBLISHING

*I dedicate this book with an abundance of thanks to Gene Balzer,
my photographer. His unerring eye and impeccable taste made
our work together an endless source of joy and wonderment.*

Artwork dimensions in photo captions refer to height or length
unless otherwise specified.
When two dimensions are given, they refer to height x width.

The display type was set in Matrix
The text type was set in AGaramond
Designed by Rudy J. Ramos
Edited by Kathleen Bryant and Erin Murphy
Production supervised by Lisa Brownfield
Manufactured in Hong Kong by
South Sea International Press Ltd.

FIRST IMPRESSION
ISBN 0-87358-673-5

Library of Congress Catalog Card Number 96-53299
Cataloging-in-Publication Data
Bassman, Theda.
    Treasures of the Navajo / Theda Bassman ;
    photographs by Gene Balzer.
        p.   cm.
    Includes bibliographical references and indexes.
        ISBN 0-87358-673-5
        1. Navajo Indians—Material culture.
        2. Navajo art. 3. Navajo Indians—Antiquities.
        I. Balzer, Gene. II. Title.
E99.Z9B335 1997
704.03'972—dc21   96-53299

0618/7.5M/4-97

OTHER BOOKS BY THEDA BASSMAN

Hopi Kachina Dolls and Their Carvers

The Kachina Dolls of Cecil Calnimptewa Their Power Their Splendor

The Beauty of Hopi Jewelry

Zuni Jewelry, which was co-authored with Michael Bassman

*Treasures of the Zuni

*Treasures of the Hopi

The Beauty of Navajo Jewelry

*Also available from Northland Publishing

Frontispiece: Storm Pattern rug, 45½ in. x 61 in., by Minnie Conn.
Courtesy of Les and Pam Jensen
Wedding basket with four large butterflies *(back),* 23½ in. high,
by Corena Fuller. *Private collection*
Wedding basket with five butterflies, 16½ in. high, by the Holiday family.
Private collection
Sandpainting of a female Yei figure, 7 in. x 13 in., by Wilfred Rotsinah.
Courtesy of Les and Pam Jensen
Pot *(left),* 10 in. high, by Alice Cling. *Private collection*
Pot *(right),* 3 in. high, by Lorraine Williams. *Private collection*
Squash blossom necklace with twenty-one Morenci turquoise stones,
artist unknown. *Courtesy R. B. Burnham & Co. Trading Post*
Bola tie with silver appliqué, twisted wire, balls, and two Stormy Mountain
turquoise stones, by Alice Platero. *Courtesy of Garland's Indian Jewelry*
Concha belt of stamped and repoussé silver work with six 3½-in. oval con-
chas, seven 3-in. butterflies, and a 3½-in. x 4½-in. buckle, by Jack Adaki.
Courtesy of Tanner's Indian Arts
Concha belt of stamped and repoussé silver work, six 3½-in. oval conchas
with nine stones of green old Persian turquoise set in each concha and
a 4½-in. buckle with seven stones, by Kee Joe Benally. *Courtesy of Tanner's
Indian Arts*
Bracelet of stamped silver 1¾-in. wide, artist unknown. *Courtesy of Santa Fe
Ranch*
Tobacco canteen of stamped silver, artist unknown. *Courtesy of Santa Fe Ranch*

Page vi, **AN ASSORTMENT OF RUGS,** *clockwise from lower left:*
Teec Nos Pos, 34½ in. x 52 in., by Marietta Joe.
Teec Nos Pos, 44 in. x 62 in., by Rachael Waters.
Teec Nos Pos, 51½ in. x 80 in., by Daisy Joe.
Teec Nos Pos with snowflake border, 35 in. x 55½ in., by Ella Henderson.
Burntwater, 33½ in. x 44 in., by Fannie Yazzie.
Teec Nos Pos, 39½ in. x 73 in., by Marjorie Nez.
Private collection

Page viii: Transition replica rug, 5 ft. x 7 ft., by Janet Tsinnie. The pattern is a copy
of a Moki design during the transition period from 1880 to 1910. *Courtesy of R. B.
Burnham & Co. Trading Post*
Squash blossom necklace *(on wedding vase)* with twisted silver wire and nineteen
turquoise stones, by Nora Tsosie. *Courtesy of Running Bear Zuni Trading Post*
Squash blossom necklace *(in pot)* with twisted silver wire, stamped
edge, silver balls, and thirty-four Fox turquoise stones, artist unknown. *Courtesy of
Turquoise Village*
Wedding vase, by Zonnie Barlow. *Courtesy of R. B. Burnham & Co. Trading Post*
Pot *(on its side),* by Christine McHorse. *Courtesy of Milford Nahohai*
Small pot, by Alice Cling. *Courtesy of Milford Nahohai*
Bracelet *(next to pot)* with stampwork and a large Bisbee turquoise stone, by Joe D.
Yazzie. *Courtesy of Al Myman*
Concha belt with six 4½-in. conchas and a 4 in. buckle, each
of stamped silver with a rectangular-cut Chinese turquoise stone,
by Calvin Martinez. *Courtesy of Running Bear Zuni Trading Post*
Overlay pendant strung on silver beads with a Chinese turquoise stone, by Tommy
Jackson. *Courtesy of Running Bear Zuni Trading Post*
Bracelet *(at top of pendant)* has stampwork and split silver wire with a single Chinese
turquoise stone, by Lorinda T. Begay. *Courtesy of Running Bear Zuni Trading Post*

CONTENTS

▼▼▼

Acknowledgments vii

Introduction 1

Jewelry 7

Pottery .19

Rugs 29

Sandpaintings 57

Paintings .67

Baskets .85

Treasures Unlimited 91

Glossary 104

Suggested Reading 106

Index of Artists 108

General Index 110

ACKNOWLEDGMENTS

▼ ▼ ▼

My thanks to the following people who so graciously permitted their treasures to be photographed:

Tony Abeyta
Antoinette and Steve Beiser
Kay Bennett
Ron and Alissa Harvey
Les and Pam Jensen
Judy Johnsen
Martin Link
Bill Malone
Al Myman
Milford Nahohai
Gary C. Newman
Ernest and Edith Schwartz
Steve and Mary Anne Sewell
Nick Smith
Emerald Tanner
Stella Tanner
Ray Tracey
And all of the private collectors who wish to remain anonymous

Additional thanks to the galleries and museums and their staffs who provided me with their treasures and help:

Andrews Pueblo Pottery,
    Albuquerque, New Mexico
R. B. Burnham & Co. Trading Post,
    Sanders, Arizona
Gallup Indian Plaza,
    Gallup, New Mexico
Garland's Indian Jewelry, Sedona, Arizona
Garland's Navajo Rugs, Sedona, Arizona
The Kaibab Shop, Tucson, Arizona
Many Hands Gallery, Sedona, Arizona
McGee's Beyond Native Tradition,
    Holbrook, Arizona
Museum of Northern Arizona Collection,
    Flagstaff, Arizona
Puchteca, Flagstaff, Arizona
Running Bear Zuni Trading Post,
    Zuni, New Mexico
Santa Fe Ranch, Palm Desert, California
Tanner's Indian Arts,
    Gallup, New Mexico
Toh-atin Gallery, Durango, Colorado
Turquoise Village, Zuni, New Mexico

Special thanks to Bruce Burnham and Martin Link who were always ready to answer my questions and to give much needed help.

As always, my gratitude to my husband, Michael, who is constantly ready to help, putting aside his own interests. I could not have written this book without his assistance and support.

Lastly, my thanks to my photographer, Gene Balzer, whose artistry makes the book come alive.

Introduction

THE DINÉ ARE the Navajo People. Navajo legend maintains that the Diné had to pass through three different worlds before emerging into the world as we know it—the Fourth World.

The Navajos believe there are the Earth People and the Holy People. The Holy People have the power to help or to harm the Earth People. The Earth People must maintain harmony or balance on Mother Earth since they are an essential segment of the universe. This harmony is known as *Hózhó*.

It is a further belief that centuries ago the Holy People taught the Navajos how to live harmoniously with Mother Earth, Father Sky, and other vital elements such as man, animals, and plants.

The Holy People designated four sacred mountains to represent the boundaries of the Navajos. White Shell Woman represents the east at Mt. Blanca, Colorado; Turquoise Woman represents the south at Mt. Taylor, New Mexico; Abalone Woman represents the west at the San Francisco Peaks, near Flagstaff, Arizona; and Jet Black Woman represents the north at Mt. Hesperus, west of Durango, Colorado.

The Navajo Nation covers eighteen million acres of unbelievable beauty and vast mineral and energy reserves, timber, and agricultural riches. With the discovery of oil in the 1920s, petroleum companies had great interest in leasing Navajo land for exploration. With the income from oil, timber, gas, and agricultural leases, the Navajo

Nation had funding for extensive governmental activities. Consequently, in 1923 a tribal government was established. Today the capital of the Navajo Nation is in Window Rock, Arizona.

The Navajo tribal government consists of three branches—executive, legislative, and judicial. It incorporates an elected tribal chairman, vice chairman, and eighty-eight council delegates representing one hundred and ten chapters throughout Navajoland. The Navajo tribal government is the largest American Indian governmental entity and is extremely sophisticated. Its main goal is to attain economic self-sufficiency for its people.

Anthropologists believe that the first Navajos arrived in the Southwest between A.D. 1000 and 1525. Their physique and language suggested a strong kinship to the Athapascan tribes of Western Canada and the interior of Alaska. They settled in the part of the Southwest now known as Four Corners, where New Mexico, Colorado, Utah, and Arizona join. They became farmers and took up weaving and sandpainting.

The population of the Navajo Nation is currently over two hundred thousand, with a projected annual growth of between two and three percent. This figure is staggering when you consider that the total Navajo population in 1868 was only eight thousand. In 1863 the United States government routed the Navajos from their homes in Canyon de Chelly, Arizona, after destroying their crops and livestock. The Navajos surrendered to Colonel Kit Carson, the officer in charge of the United States Army

troops. The Navajos were marched approximately four hundred miles from Fort Defiance, Arizona, to Bosque Redondo, an internment camp outside Fort Sumner, New Mexico. The first Navajo prisoners began the Long Walk from Fort Defiance in late 1863. In the spring of 1864 the remainder of the eighty-five hundred Navajo prisoners was marched to Bosque Redondo. After four years of imprisonment, the Navajos were allowed to resettle in their own lands. By this time the Navajos had been reduced to the startlingly low number of eight thousand, as many of them died on the Long Walk and many more died in the camp.

In the early 1870s traders emerged on the reservation. Their trading posts provided a place where Indians could sell their goods and receive goods in return. The trading post became the social center of the area. The Navajos sold wool from their sheep in the spring and lambs in the autumn to the post. They also brought in their rugs and jewelry to sell to the traders and often pawned their personal belongings. The successful trader learned the Navajo language, knew and respected their religion, and understood their beliefs and taboos. He acted as an advisor, confidant, and mortician. He helped in reading letters and filling out government forms. Often, he married into the tribe. He believed in looking after the material welfare of his neighbors, and in finding the best market prices for their artwork. At the same time, the trader did not forget that he himself was in business to make a fair profit. Above all, the trader had to establish a reputation of complete honesty or he would soon be out of business. Word of mouth from one Indian to others traveled fast. In short, the accepted trader believed in the dignity of people, and that the Navajos were entitled to equality and respect. The credo of the trader was that for him to prosper, the Indian must prosper.

John Lorenzo Hubbell was the prototype of the "modern" trader. The Hubbell Trading Post, located just west of the Navajo community in Ganado, Arizona, on State Highway 264, is the home of one of the nation's oldest trading posts. Many Navajos still purchase groceries and other dry goods there today. Of course, they bring in their rugs and jewelry to sell, and jewelry to put in to pawn.

On April 3, 1967, Hubbell Trading Post was purchased by the United States government to be operated as a National Historic Site. The original purpose of trading with the Indians is still in effect. Bill Malone, the manager of Hubbell's Trading Post, is carrying on the traditions of John Lorenzo Hubbell. The historic site attracts thousands of Navajos and hundreds of thousands of non-Navajo visitors each year. In addition, a group called Friends of Lorenzo Hubbell has been formed by Martin Link and others to offer the National Park Service assistance in preserving the trading post's heritage. In these ways an important record of the trading post's history is being accurately saved.

There have been other significant changes

on the Navajo Reservation. The Navajos used to depend on the horse and wagon for transportation. Now most of them have pickup trucks and paved roads, making it easier to get to nearby towns for shopping and the selling of rugs, jewelry, and sandpaintings. Modern transportation has certainly had an impact on the survival of many trading posts. For the Navajos, the acquisition of a truck is often an extended family affair. Adult members of a family will pool their income resources in order to make monthly payments. Truck payments are usually the largest singular household expense.

Housing has also changed. The majority of Navajos used to live in hogans, a six- or eight-sided one-room home for the entire family. Today most people build their own homes or live in government-subsidized housing.

In addition to raising livestock, the Diné now earn a living working for wages in industries developed on the reservation, such as forestry, mining, manufacturing, and construction, as well as government work and tourism. People also move off the reservation to work in nearby cities and towns. Another means of support is the creating of artwork such as rugs, jewelry, sandpaintings, pottery, paintings, and baskets. These activities are usually reservation based. The Navajo artist is tremendously talented in creating exquisite and multifaceted works of art.

An interesting chapter in Navajo history involves the use of approximately four hundred Navajo men as Code Talkers while in

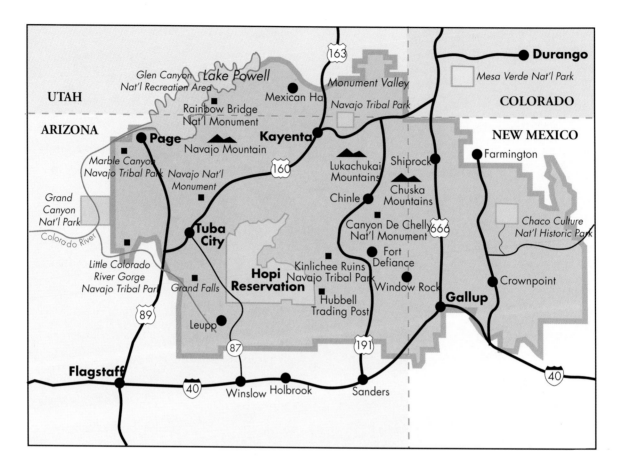

the United States Marine Corps in World War II. Navajo was one of the world's hidden languages at that time, as it had no written form, no alphabet, nor other symbols. The Navajo "code" was the only code never deciphered by the Japanese, allowing Marines to send secret messages that helped to win the war in the Pacific. The Navajo Code Talkers were equipped with the only foolproof, unbreakable code in the history of warfare.

Since the beginning of their history, the well-being of the Navajo people has been entrusted to the medicine men. Today there are about seven hundred medicine men, and their ranks are diminishing rapidly. More and more young Navajos are opting for an Anglo lifestyle. There is a growing fear

among tribal leaders that the days of the medicine man may soon be over. Even though young Navajos do not want to be medicine men, a few programs at the Navajo Community College still provide financial aid to those who wish to study to become a medicine man or woman.

Many important chants or ways are conducted by the medicine man, who is known as a singer. He is actually a priest-practitioner. One of these chants is the Yei-bi-chai Dance, which is another name for Night Chant or Night Way. It is a major winter curing ceremony, performed to heal the patient of stress and other related ailments.

The name Yei-bi-chai is used for the Night Way because numerous Yeis appear during the last two nights of the nine-day ceremony. Yeis are the masked representations of supernatural beings who possess great powers.

On the eighth night the Yei-bi-chais initiate young Navajo girls and boys in order to introduce them to the secret of the masked gods. On the ninth and last night of the Way, Yei-bi-chai dance teams perform, each group singing in the falsetto voice for which the dancers are noted. It is a dramatic finale.

Another important ceremony, the Entah or Enemy Way, is referred to as Squaw Dance by non-Indians. It is conducted only in summer months for persons whose sickness has been diagnosed as resulting from contact with Anglos or other non-Navajos.

The Enemy Way is a three-day ritual that begins at the patient's hogan and moves to a different location on each successive day. On the third day, the Black Dancers, who are the clowns of the War Ceremony, perform a Mud Dance in which the patient and then some of the spectators are caught and playfully given a mud bath, much to the pleasure of those not seized by the clowns.

The Squaw Dance is performed on the third night of the Enemy Way. It is primarily a coming-out event for eligible young females, who invite young men to join them in a round dance. As the dance progresses the young women usually get bolder and become the leaders of the dance. After several rounds the man is required to make token payment to the girl for the privilege of dancing with her. The Squaw Dance lasts all night, and it is performed to the accompaniment of a chorus and a drummer.

Many Navajos have become Christians. Almost every Christian denomination is active on the reservation. The Church of Jesus Christ of Latter-day Saints has the largest membership.

In the 1930s the Native American Church promoted belief in the Christian religion with the practice of the Peyote Sacrament for its members. The church believes that members, through the chewing of peyote, can hallucinate and can overcome inhibitions and say what is really troubling them. The peyote acts as a purifier as well. National membership of the Native American Church is 450,000 and Navajo membership totals about 20,000. The church won a long battle in the courts for the legalization of the use of peyote for religious purposes only.

The Navajos live close to their Pueblo neighbors and have borrowed many cultural elements from the Hopis and Zunis. They learned about the use of silver from their Mexican neighbors. Even though the Navajos have borrowed art forms, they have elaborated on them so that the final product is distinctively their own. In the weaving of rugs, for example, the Navajo's finished work is more elaborate and superior to the textile work they learned from the Pueblos. The Navajos have created beautiful enduring art treasures.

Jewelry

IN 1850 A Navajo medicine man, Atsidi Sani, became the first Navajo to make silver jewelry. He was taught by a Mexican blacksmith.

Initially Atsidi Sani and several other Navajos made silver jewelry only for themselves, for their personal wear and the adornment of their families. Even though they may have made pieces to trade on occasion with their neighbors for livestock, few Navajos made jewelry as a livelihood. They were not considered professional silversmiths.

Bracelet with cluster of Sleeping Beauty turquoise, by A. Jake.

Bola tie, ring, and pendant with clusters of Chinese turquoise, artists unknown.

Leather ketoh of textured silver overlaid with silver lines and dots and set with five Kingman turquoise stones, artist unknown.

Courtesy McGee's Beyond Native Tradition

Throughout their history, however, the Navajos have learned to take the best of a foreign culture and combine it with their own talents. They began to master the art of silversmithing from the Pueblos, the Spanish, and their Mexican neighbors. Ironically, silversmithing skills may have spread among the Navajos during their 1864–1868 internment at Bosque Redondo, one of the bleakest periods of their history. Indications are that a number of Navajos learned the rudiments of silversmithing at the blacksmith shop at Bosque Redondo.

The number of Navajos who produced silver work remained small. Their work was highly regarded and sought after by other Navajos. In fact, silver jewelry became a status symbol of a man's wealth and his reputation in the community.

In 1884, the owner of Hubbell Trading Post in Ganado, Arizona, hired two Mexican silversmiths to teach Navajos to solder and work with silver. The results of this early apprenticeship emphasized the heavy use of metals, with few stones and a simplicity of design.

To obtain metal, the Navajos melted American silver coins, then beat the molten silver to make jewelry. However, in 1890 the Currency Defacement Act was passed by the Congress of the United States, prohibiting the use of American coins in this manner. The Navajos turned to the softer Mexican silver coins as an alternate silver supply.

It was not long before the main characteristic of Navajo jewelry involved the use of silver with an accent of turquoise or coral stones. For design and decoration the Navajo silversmith resorted to stampwork, engraving, and the use of filigree. Elaborate silver designs soon replaced the simplicity of earlier designs. They became a hallmark of Navajo originality.

After all the Navajos were released from Fort Sumner in 1868 and returned to a reservation area, the United States government established a merchandising system to provide the Navajos with items they needed and had no way of obtaining—food, clothing, and everyday supplies. This was accomplished by using the trading posts as conduits. For years the trading post was the only contact the Navajos and other Indians had with the white man. With the passage of time there was a development of skills and usage of better tools. The Navajos pro-

duced more delicate work. They also used many stones to greater advantage and beauty, where formerly few stones sufficed.

Several designs or items are distinctively Navajo. The squash blossom necklace blends fine, round silver beads with beads suggestive of the pomegranate flower, a design that adorned the clothes of Spanish and Mexican gentlemen. Attached to the beads is the *naja,* a crescent-shaped pendant, originally a talisman fastened to the horse's bridle. The Spanish brought this good luck omen to the New World. Another Navajo specialty inspired by Spanish design is the concha belt, a favorite adornment of Navajo men and a major object for displaying the imagination and skill of the silverworker. The concha belt has elegance and class. The *ketoh,* or bow guard (sometimes spelled *gato*), is a Navajo innovation. When the bow and arrow were in use, the archer needed a way to protect his wrist from the stinging snap of the bowstring. The archer used bow guards made of leather with little ornamentation. The Navajo silversmith made the ketoh into an object of striking design and beauty. The leather was decorated with stunning designs on attached silver plates. Many Navajo men wear ketohs purely for pleasure, since the bow and arrow are no longer used. The Hopis and Zunis wear the Navajo-made ketoh in their ceremonial dances. All three of these items—the squash blossom necklace, the concha belt, and the ketoh—are classic Navajo style.

Turquoise was first used as an accent with silver in the early 1880s. By the end of the nineteenth century, trader Don Lorenzo

Hubbell, seeing the meteoric rise in the popularity of the turquoise stones, imported Persian turquoise for trade to the Navajos. Persian turquoise was clear, blue, and known worldwide for its beauty and desirability. Shortly after 1890 a number of turquoise-producing mines opened in the Four Corners region, resulting in a significant flow of turquoise to the trading posts of the Southwest.

The creating of silver and turquoise jewelry became widespread by the early years of the twentieth century. Originally, it was the Navajo men who fashioned jewelry. However, Navajo women began working the metal and turquoise as well when it became evident that there was an economic advantage to be gained by the family working together. The Navajos saw the initial glimmers of possibility in making jewelry as a livelihood.

Over the years jewelry has served three main purposes for the Navajos: (1) They wear jewelry to display their wealth. It is not a question of exhibiting personal wealth, but rather of revealing to the people at large ceremonial gatherings, for example, what wealth the family has. (2) They enjoy the beauty of the jewelry, its decorativeness, and the good feelings derived from wearing it. (3) They use the jewelry as collateral in trading posts, against which they can borrow in exchange for goods or money. This is called pawn.

Pawn became part of the Navajo culture. The Navajos prefer to use their jewelry as wealth, since an item can be pawned over and over again. During ceremonial gather-

ings the Navajos bedeck themselves with turquoise jewelry. This is one of the occasions they take their jewelry out of pawn, only to put it back in after the ceremony. Sometimes they will put the jewelry into pawn as a safekeeping measure, rather than leave it in the hogan. The owner of the jewelry has a specified time period in which to reclaim the jewelry before it becomes dead pawn and is made available to the public for sale. It is estimated that over the years only ten percent of the jewelry ends up as dead pawn.

The question of quality arises from the pawn system. Is an item of jewelry good because it has been in pawn? Is it good, or valuable, because it is old? Age alone is no criterion of art. The best of the old will always be prime, as will the best of the contemporary. It is foolhardy to value a second-rate piece of work more highly simply because it is old, rather than because it is well-crafted and aesthetically pleasing.

Of all the Southwestern tribes, the Navajos endow turquoise with the highest social, economic, and religious importance. Turquoise is the most important ornamental stone in ceremonials, and it is often referred to in Navajo myths and tales. The turquoise of today comes not only from the mines of the Southwest but also from Australia, China, Chile, Mexico, Persia, and Tibet.

Materials, methods, and styles in Navajo jewelry making have changed in many ways in the last hundred years. While early jewelers used silver exclusively, Navajo jewelry making evolved to include turquoise and coral, and then a magnificent array of stones, shells, and gems. The galaxy of materials used today includes azurite, charoite, angel coral, oxblood coral, salmon coral, diamonds, dolomite, emeralds, fossilized ivory, gold, ironwood, jet, lapis lazuli, malachite, onyx, Australian white and black opal, pearls, Royal Web Gemstone, rubies, spiny oyster shell, and sugilite. In technique there is more innovation, originality, and quality in workmanship, with a fineness of design and symmetry. Much of the work falls in the category of contemporary, and yet a number of the artists who make this kind of jewelry maintain that the inspiration is traditional.

Some of the prominent jewelers are Julian Arviso, Calvin Begay, Betty and Billy Betoney, Tommy Jackson, Jesse Monongye, Wilbert Muskett, Jr., Gibson Nez, Boyd Tsosie, Ray Tracey, Lee Yazzie, and numerous others.

Though their backgrounds vary—some are young, some are older, some are contemporary, some are traditional—they are all hardworking. Above all, they are talented artisans who have given of themselves in unique ways.

People buy Native American jewelry for a myriad of reasons. They should buy only what they truly like. Any jewelry that is handmade with high quality of workmanship and material will always give its wearer enjoyment and pleasure. Good Indian jewelry is timeless and looks wonderful worn—day or night. However, the greatest value of Native American jewelry is its inherent beauty.

NOTE: *All jewelry is sterling silver unless otherwise noted. All gold jewelry is 14-karat unless otherwise noted.*

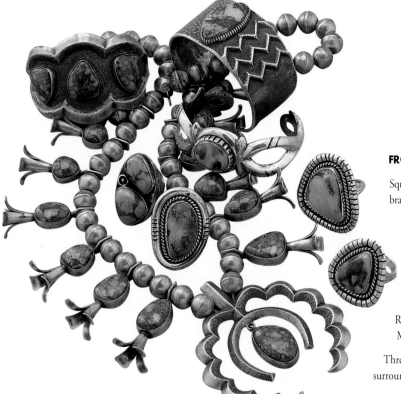

FROM YEARS PAST:

Squash blossom necklace with cast pendant and matching bracelet, both with Montezuma Nevada turquoise, by Della and Francis James.

Tufa cast bracelet *(upper right)* with a Royston turquoise stone, by Herman Coan.

Tufa cast bracelet, below, with a Battle Mountain turquoise stone, by Betty Rose Billie.

Ring with stamped silver balls and two stones of Battle Mountain turquoise, by Wilson Tsosie.

Three rings with stamped edges and twisted rope borders surrounding single Royston turquoise stones, by Ed Shirley.

All made in the 1970s. *Courtesy of Tanner's Indian Arts*

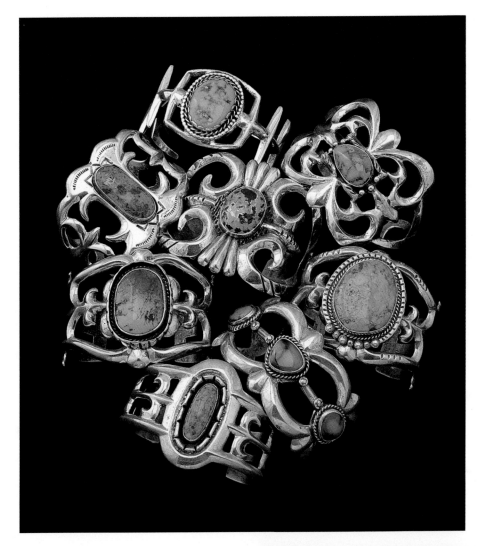

CAST BRACELETS FROM YEARS PAST,
clockwise from upper left:

With Morenci turquoise stone, by Maggie Betsie.

With Royston turquoise stone, by Eugene Jackson.

With Bisbee turquoise stone, by Evelyn Anderson.

With three Bisbee turquoise stones,
by Betty Rose Billie.

With Persian turquoise stone, by Benjamin Murphy.

With Bisbee turquoise stone, by Maggie Betsie.

With Persian turquoise stone, by Maggie Betsie.

Center: With Persian turquoise stone,
by Maggie Betsie.

All made in the 1970s. *Courtesy of Tanner's Indian Arts*

GOLD BRACELETS:

Clockwise from top center: Beveled, mosaic,
and channel inlay China Mountain turquoise,
lapis lazuli, and ironwood, by Julian Arviso.

Inlay of China Mountain turquoise, by Leon Ashley.

Beveled, mosaic, and channel inlay China
Mountain turquoise, red coral, ironwood,
and lapis lazuli, by Julian Arviso.

Beveled, mosaic coral and turquoise, by David Clark.

Mosaic and channel inlay lapis lazuli and opal,
by Julian Arviso.

Beveled, mosaic, and channel inlay lapis lazuli
and pink coral, by Julian Arviso.

Beveled, mosaic, and channel inlay China
Mountain turquoise, opal, fossilized ivory,
coral, and jet, by Julian Arviso.

Courtesy of Gallup Indian Plaza

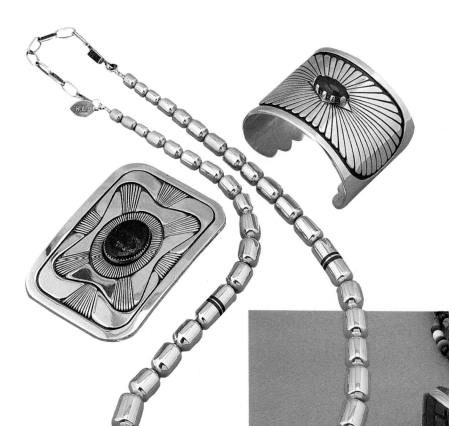

LEFT: Belt buckle of stamped overlay silver with lapis lazuli stone, by Gibson Nez.

Necklace of handmade graduated silver barrel beads inlaid with lapis lazuli stones, by Henry Lee Smith.

Bracelet of stamped overlay silver with lapis lazuli stone, by Deborah Silversmith.

Courtesy of Many Hands Gallery

SOMETHING DIFFERENT:

Necklace *(left)* with beads of lapis lazuli, spiny oyster shell, coral, sugilite, and silver, and side pendant of mosaic inlay, by Tommy Jackson.

Necklace *(right)* with beads of lapis lazuli, spiny oyster shell, turquoise, jet, sugilite, dolomite, and silver, and side pendant of mosaic inlay, by Edison Iskeets.

Bracelet *(upper right)* with sugilite, by Dererie Yellowhorse.

Bracelet *(lower left)* with lapis lazuli and coral, by Dererie Yellowhorse.

Courtesy of Many Hands Gallery

SOMETHING DIFFERENT, *left to right:*

Concha belt with twelve conchas, each 3 in. x 2 in. with fifty-seven needlepoint turquoise stones.

String tie with forty-five petit point turquoise stones.

Watch tips with thirty-two petit point turquoise stones.

Tie with twenty-seven diamond-cut and two petit point turquoise stones.

Ranger belt buckle with fourteen petit point and two round turquoise stones.

All made by Betty and Billy Betoney. All turquoise is Sleeping Beauty. *Courtesy of Garland's Indian Jewelry*

LINKED CONCHA BELTS, *top to bottom:*

Twelve conchas, each 3 in. x 2 in., with engraved keystone shape, by Alverez Perez.

Sixteen oval conchas, each 1½ in. x 1 in., with stamped shadow box design and Sleeping Beauty turquoise, by Allison Lee.

Sixteen conchas, each 1¾ in. x 1⅜ in., with stampwork and coral stones, by Emmett Nelson.

Twelve dome-shaped conchas, each 2¼ in. diameter, with stamped Navajo wedding basket design, artist unknown.

Courtesy of Garland's Indian Jewelry

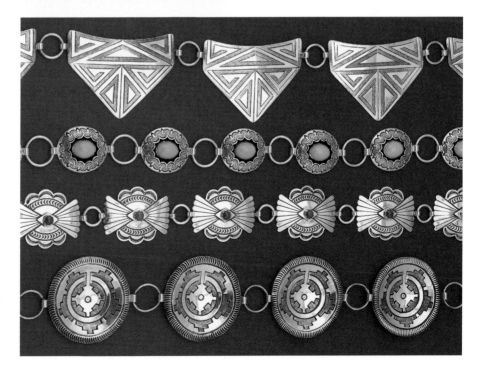

ALL 14-KARAT GOLD:

Necklace with hand-rolled lapis lazuli, Australian opal, oxblood coral, turquoise, and gold beads, and reversible bear pendant, by Jesse Monongye. The facing side of the pendant is made of Australian opal, lapis lazuli, salmon and oxblood coral, sugilite, and turquoise. The reverse side is made of lapis lazuli, dolomite, gold lip mother-of-pearl, oxblood coral, sugilite, and turquoise. This won Best of Show at the Gallup Inter-Tribal Indian Ceremonial in Gallup, New Mexico, in 1991.

Cast bracelet, gold work by Calvin Begay, with mosaic and channel inlay of sugilite, Australian opal, and turquoise set by Wilbert Muskett, Jr.

Ring, gold work by Rick Tolino, with mosaic inlay of lapis lazuli and Australian opal set by Wilbert Muskett, Jr.

Earrings, gold work by Calvin Begay, with mosaic inlay of turquoise, Australian opal, and sugilite set by Wilbert Muskett, Jr.

Courtesy of Garland's Indian Jewelry

GOLD ON SILVER:

UPPER ROW, *left to right:* Swirl earrings, by Howard Nelson.

Ring with Flute Players and two rings with bears, overlay with textured background, by Robert Taylor.

CENTER ROW, *left to right:* Belt buckle with Flute Players, overlay and stampwork, by Robert Taylor.

Belt buckle with ketoh design, overlay and stampwork, by Howard Nelson.

LOWER ROW, *left to right:* Navajo story bracelet with hogan, wood stack, and horses in overlay and stampwork, by Francis Tabaha.

Navajo story bracelet with Monument Valley scene in overlay and stampwork, by Robert Taylor.

Courtesy of McGee's Beyond Native Tradition

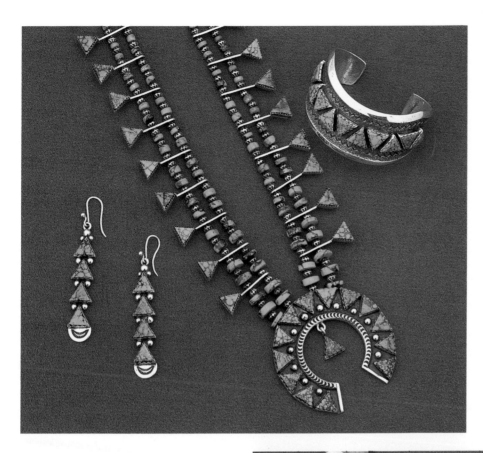

Variation of a squash blossom necklace with silver stampwork and triangular Chinese turquoise stones, strung with fluted silver and turquoise beads, with matching turquoise earrings and cast bracelet, by Chester Kahn. *Courtesy of Tanner's Indian Arts*

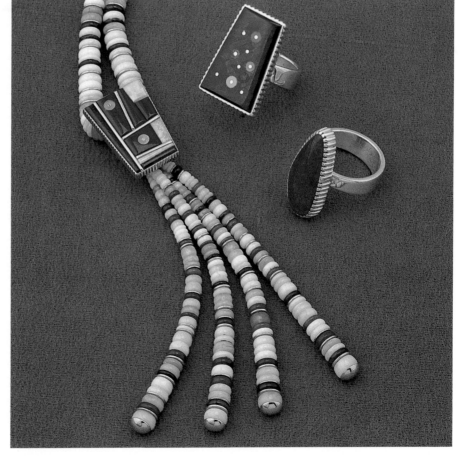

Necklace with Australian white and black opal, sugilite, and gold beads and pendant of beveled, mosaic, and channel inlay using the same stones set in 14-karat gold. *Private collection*

Silver ring inlaid with sugilite, angel and oxblood coral, turquoise, and gold circles. *Courtesy of Garland's Indian Jewelry*

Silver ring with a single sugilite stone. *Courtesy of Garland's Indian Jewelry*

All made by Boyd Tsosie.

Five-strand necklace of tubular coral with olivella shell heishe and matching mosaic bracelet with beveled coral stones, by Mary Marie Yazzie.

Concha belt of stamped silver on leather with nine 1½-in. x 1¾-in. conchas and a buckle, each with a coral stone, and butterfly symbols, by Kee Joe Benally.

Stamped silver ranger belt buckle with coral stones, by Kee Joe Benally.

Courtesy of Tanner's Indian Arts

ROYAL WEB GEMSTONE:

Concha belt with a cast butterfly belt buckle and seven inlaid butterfly-shaped conchas, each 1¾ in. x 1½ in., by Chester Kahn.

Bola tie and matching belt buckle *(top)* with stampwork and repoussé, by Kee Joe Benally.

Necklace with fluted and round silver beads and a cast pendant of a Butterfly Maiden Kachina inlaid with Royal Web Gemstone, coral, jet, and white mother-of-pearl, by Nuesie and George Henry.

Bracelet with a gold **T** and beveled Royal Web Gemstone, by Raymond Yazzie.

Ranger belt buckle with stampwork *(lower left),* by Chester Kahn.

Cast belt buckle *(lower right),* by Lee Yazzie.

All courtesy of Tanner's Indian Arts except bracelet, courtesy of Stella Tanner

Old-style squash blossom necklace with silver stampwork and a triangular cut Indian Mountain turquoise stone on the naja, by Ray Tracey. The clasp has an oval Indian Mountain turquoise stone and can be removed and used as a pin.

Courtesy of the artist

Pottery

FOR MANY YEARS the Navajos made pottery for their own domestic use and for ceremonial activities. With the arrival of the trading posts, the Navajos were able to obtain better utensils made of metal and glass for their own consumption. Young women, who would ordinarily learn pottery-making skills from their mothers and aunts, became disinterested and disenchanted in making their own household utensils.

Left to right: Pot with village scene (with petroglyphs, not shown), 14½ in. high, entitled *Echoes of Ancients.* *Courtesy of McGee's Beyond Native Tradition*

Pot with handle, Yei-bi-chai Dancers, and cloud symbols, 9½ in. high, made in 1973. *Private collection*

Pot entitled *Yei-bi-chai Dancers,* 17¼ in. high. *Courtesy of McGee's Beyond Native Tradition*

All made by Lucy Leuppe McKelvey.

In addition, no commercial market for pottery existed. It was less trouble to barter for these goods at the trading post. These manufactured goods slowly and inevitably replaced the need for Navajo clay vessels.

Subsequently, the domestic consumption of pottery declined tremendously, though Navajo ceremonialism provided an outlet for much of the pottery production. Affecting production were many taboos and restrictions imposed on the potter by the traditionalists and medicine men of the tribe. They told the potter that she should not allow anyone to watch her at work, that she should not have bad thoughts about others, and that she should not make pottery if she were menstruating. The restrictive list went on and on, and those who told her how to behave acted as judge and jury. They assured her that any pottery cracking or breakage was the consequence of her transgression. They also suggested that the errant potter may suffer illnesses or accidents. It isn't surprising that in a total Navajo population of over two hundred thousand, only two hundred or so potters are willing to risk the slings and arrows of the "guardians," their detractors. Moreover, in terms of aesthetics Navajo pots certainly could not compete with Pueblo wares in the commercial market. With all these negatives, it was no wonder that the craft of Navajo pottery was doomed to fail.

In spite of the decline in the Navajo domestic market for pottery, the demand for pottery in ceremonial use increased. This was probably the prime reason the craft was kept alive into the 1950s. Prior to this time, Navajo pottery was characteristically crude and not very aesthetically pleasing.

Today, there is a revival of Navajo pottery making, centering in the Shonto–Cow Springs area of the Navajo reservation in Arizona. There is also a difference in the quality of the work—it is more attractive, it is more colorful, it is more artistic.

The Shonto–Cow Springs area is also home to the best clay. The potter is usually able to tell how good the clay bed is by its texture or color. The clay is usually hard and has to be broken into small pieces with a hammer. Sometimes the clay is pounded or is ground into fine particles on a metate, a grinding stone. The potter adds water to the ground clay and soaks the mixture until it can be easily worked. At this time she removes by hand all foreign impurities—small rock particles, small slivers of wood, or roots.

Then follows the process of adding temper to strengthen the clay and prevent cracking during the firing. For tempering, most potters use crushed pottery shards. Some use volcanic cinder, while a lesser number prefer sand.

The potter uses the traditional coil-and-scrape method to construct a vessel. She makes a base by kneading the clay into her envisioned shape. Then she makes coils of clay, usually between a quarter-inch and a half-inch thick, and builds on the base one coil at a time. As a coil is added, she scrapes the line between it and the previous coil until it is smooth, using the traditional burnt corncob or a smooth wooden stick. The potter moistens each coil with water, rubbing with the stick or corncob until the small cracks are filled and the surface irregularities are leveled out. After she builds the vessel to the desired shape, she allows it to dry in order to remove all excessive moisture from the clay. Failure to get rid of that moisture may result in the pot cracking or peeling during the firing.

The firing is usually done in a pit located near the hogan. The potter places the thoroughly dried vessel on a bed of warm coals. Then she piles an ample amount of wood and sheep dung around and over the vessel. She ignites the fire and allows it to burn down. Firing time is as little as a half hour or as much as an hour or more, depending upon the size of the vessel and the watchful eye of the potter. She knows when the pot is done. After the fire burns down she sometimes leaves the pot in the coals, allowing it to cool down gradually to minimize the risk of cracking.

When she takes the pot out of the pit, the potter will hold it in one hand and gently snap the top of a finger of her other hand against the wall of the vessel. If there is a resonant, pinging sound, the potter will inwardly smile. There is no crack. Incidentally, the prospective buyer or collector of pottery should use this technique before purchasing a desired piece. Love the pot, love the price, then test. A dull, thudding sound is a no-no!

Sometimes during firing, pieces of the hot fuel—coal or dung—will come in contact with the vessel, creating dark, discolored areas on the surface of the pot. Pueblo potters try to avoid these fire clouds, but many Navajo potters seem to find them attractive. As a buyer, let your own eye and judgment be the final criteria.

The application of one or more coats of melted pinyon pitch is the final step in the completion of a vessel. The applied pitch provides Navajo pottery with its distinguishing shiny appearance and dark brown coloration.

The contemporary Navajo potter uses several decorating and finishing techniques. The most widely used technique is *appliqué*—the addition of clay to the exterior finish of a pot that for all practical purposes is finished. The clay might be shaped as an oak leaf, a flower, a horned toad or frog, or most often as a clay band known as a decorative fillet. The fillet forms a circle around the vessel just below the rim. Its ends are not joined, creating a ceremonial break in the design, similar to the "spirit line" incorporated into some Navajo rugs, wedding baskets, or sandpaintings. The spirit line prevents the artist from being trapped in that one particular item, providing a "way out" so that he or she can go on to make additional rugs, wedding baskets, sandpaintings, or pots.

Modeling is a technique in which the potter creates a decoration by scraping together or mounding the clay from the actual walls of the pottery.

Incising is a technique in which the potter draws a pointed stick through the wet clay surface of the pottery to make an accent of shallow lines.

The *stamping* technique is accomplished with a fingernail, the blunt end of a stick, or the use of die tools, such as those used by the silversmith. The instrument is pressed into the soft clay. When withdrawn, it leaves an impression. Repeated pressing often results in lovely flower designs.

Carving is a technique that very few Navajo potters use. Carving involves the removal of a part of the clay from the vessel. It is very much like sculpting, and it produces not only geometric design, but also interesting scenes of recessed cliff-dwellings, women tending their sheep, or horses in a corral.

The forms and shapes of Navajo pottery include bowls, cooking jars, pipes, wedding vases, multi-spouted jars, effigy figurines, sandpainted jars, replicas of iron skillets, and tureens. The drum pot is a popular item. The potter makes the ceramic portion of the drum; the drum head is a small piece of hide that is stretched tautly over the mouth of the jar and tied with rawhide. Striking the drum head creates a lovely resonant tone. Demand for drum pots for ceremonial use is so great that very few of them are available in commercial, non-Navajo outlets.

As stated earlier, while the demand for Navajo pottery for personal, domestic consumption declined, the demand for Navajo ceremonial pottery rose dramatically. There was also a heightened interest in the non-Navajo commercial market for some of the pots with simple, yet sophisticated painted, designs.

There are a number of excellent contemporary potters. Alice Williams Cling of Shonto produces pottery that is simple, yet graceful. Her surfaces have a soft sheen, and her burnishing technique is exciting. Alice is one of the potters who uses fire clouds to enhance the looks of her pottery.

Betty Manygoats of the Shonto–Cow Springs area pots both large and small pieces. She makes effigy vessels, animal figurines, and wedding vases. Her large wedding vases are sixteen inches or more in height and are decorated with dozens of appliquéd horned toads—awesome works of beauty! She is one of the few potters who paints some of her appliquéd motifs.

Since the family is the most important unit in Navajo society, it was a natural development that many family members began to participate in the overall pottery-making procedure. Faye Tso of Tuba City is a noted medicine woman and activist in Navajo issues. Faye, her husband Emmett, and several of their daughters are accomplished potters. Their style features pottery with bold appliqués of Yei-bi-chai figures or ears of corn with floating husks.

Bertha and Silas Claw are wife and husband potters. Bertha is noted for her thin-walled cooking jars, wedding vases, and triple-spouted jars. She decorates the cooking jars with a "necklace" at the rim, creating works of simple elegance. She finishes her jars with a pinyon pitch coating.

Silas Claw does multi-spouted vessels, which he decorates with appliquéd and incised motifs. He is also skillful in the making of elaborate effigy pipe bowls. He applies oil paints to parts of the appliqués and coats his large spouted vessels with varnish.

Several potters reflect Pueblo influences, including Ida Sahmie, Nathan Begaye, Christine McHorse, and Lucy Leuppe McKelvey, to cite a few. Yet, their designs and motifs are distinctly Navajo in character.

Lucy Leuppe McKelvey has been making pottery for over twenty-two years. She is recognized for her large vessels displaying elaborate geometric designs and life-form figures, such as the sacred Yeis and Yei-bi-chais. Her painting style and technique are magnificent.

She has been criticized by some Navajos for using the Yei and Yei-bi-chai figures on her pottery. However, she feels that since her pottery making is very personal, she has the right to choose which designs to use, as long as she is true to her goal of keeping the Navajo culture alive. She feels sad that her grandfather, James Peter, and her uncle, Windway Medicine Man, left this earth without training their sons to be medicine men. To Lucy McKelvey this was losing part of their culture. She feels that painting sacred figures on her pottery is no different from the sandpainter who puts similar figures on a board and sells it as a sandpainting. To her, both are enriching the Navajo culture. She states that her designs are authentic, and it is her wish that people

know the Navajos are very much alive and growing. On a more personal level, Lucy has taught her three daughters—Cecilia, Celeste, and Celinda—the rudiments of pottery making, and all of them are producing striking pottery.

Despite many adverse influences Navajo pottery is not dying. It is as alive and vital as these potters, who continue to explore and experiment with new ideas. The commercial market for Navajo pottery has expanded beyond the confines of the trading post and retail outlets in nearby communities, reaching into the fine art galleries and museum gift shops across the entire country. Navajo pottery will probably never attain the popularity of the painted pottery of the Hopi or Rio Grande pueblos. However, it is enormously satisfying to witness the reawakening of a craft that only forty to fifty years ago was on the verge of extinction.

FROM YEARS PAST, *clockwise from top:*

Gray and yellow pot, 7 in. high, made circa 1925, artist unknown. Interior and exterior are covered with pitch, and commercial twine is tied around neck.

Red bowl with black triangles on outer rim, 7½ in. high x 9 1/2 in. diameter, pre-1902, artist unknown.

Pitch-covered pot with two coiled handles, appliquéd around rim with scallop and on both sides with acorn and double leaf design, 7 in. high x 6 in. wide, made in 1971 by Silas B. Claw.

Black pitch pot with handle, 6⅝ in. high, made circa 1935, artist unknown.

Red bowl with black rectangles, 7½ in. high x 9½ in. diameter, made circa 1900, artist unknown.

Courtesy of Museum of Northern Arizona Collection

KILN-FIRED POTTERY:

Pots made by Doreen and Roger Nelson using a potter's wheel and fired in a kiln are *(left)* with ram and feathers, 5¾ in. diameter, and *(right)* with bear, feathers, and a Bisbee turquoise stone, 7½ in. diameter.

JEWELRY, *left to right:* Bracelet with five stones of oxblood coral, by Dan Jackson.

Bracelet with six stones of salmon coral, by Orville Tsinnie.

Bracelet with six stones of oxblood coral, by Dan Jackson.

Bracelet with nine stones of salmon coral, by Orville Tsinnie.

Coin necklace *(below)* with silver dollars, half dollars, quarters, nickels, and dimes, dating from 1922 to 1944, by Louise McCabe.

Courtesy of Many Hands Gallery

Clockwise from left:

Incised geometric, 12½ in. high x 14 in. wide, by Lorraine Williams. This won Second Prize at the Museum of Northern Arizona Navajo Show in Flagstaff, Arizona, in 1992.

Vase with fire clouds, 9 in. high, by Samuel Many Mules.

Two incised geometric pots, 5½ in. high x 5¼ in. wide, by Lorraine Williams.

Courtesy of The Kaibab Shop

Clockwise from top center: Wedding vase with appliquéd toad, 7 in. high, by Betty Manygoats.

Pot with fire clouds, 7¼ in. high, by Betty Manygoats.

Incised geometric, 3¼ in. high, by Lorraine Williams.

Coiled pot with interior and exterior covered with pitch, 2½ in. high, by Stella Goodman.

Pot with kiva steps and fire clouds, 3¾ in. high, by Lorenzo Spencer.

Pot with appliquéd corn, 3½ in. high, by Tina Tso.

Etched designs and fire clouds, 11 in. high, by Faye Tso.

CENTER: Canteen with two appliquéd turtles, 6½ in. high, by Myra Tso.

Courtesy of Andrews Pueblo Pottery

Clockwise from far right: Orange pot with fire clouds, 7¼ in. high, by Alice Cling.

Orange pot with incised eagle designs, 3 in. high x 7½ in. wide, signed SAW.

Orange square-mouthed pot covered with black, 6 in. high, by Susie Crank.

Red pot with incised triangular designs and fire clouds, 5¼ in. high, by Alice Cling.

Red pot with incised triangular designs and fire clouds, 6¾ in. high, by Alice Cling.

Courtesy of Puchteca

Rugs

WHEN ONE THINKS of the Navajos, one visualizes Navajo rugs. The bold red background of the Ganado rug is accented by a central diamond shape with a black, white, and gray design. Zigzags, geometric patterns, and crosses adorn the corners of the dark-bordered rug. Many view the Ganado rug as the classic Navajo weaving. All Navajo rugs are considered tapestries due to the tightness of the weave.

The Burntwater rug has a combination of earth tones and pastels. Its color range includes the warmth of mustard, sienna, and rust and the soft pastels of rose, blue,

FROM YEARS PAST:

A collection of J. B. Moore rugs dating 1900–1920, all woven from natural, combed, homespun wool and aniline dyes. *Courtesy of Tanner's Indian Arts*

lilac, and green. It is multibordered, and the design elements favor geometrics, triangles, diagonals, and exciting Teec Nos Pos designs.

The Two Grey Hills rug has a white, gray, and black design. The handspun wool is natural (not dyed), although the black may have some dye added. The wool is very fine, and many Two Grey Hills rugs are woven as incredible tapestries with as many as 115 wefts to the inch. By comparison, a good Navajo rug in another style will have thirty or more wefts to the inch. As a consequence, a handsome Two Grey Hills rug will command premium prices. The late Daisy Tauglechee was the foremost weaver of Two Grey Hills rugs.

The Teec Nos Pos rug is bold, with Persian-looking designs. It is multicolored and has an involved, complicated center with decorative arrows and feathers emanating from it. It has either a single dark border or multiple borders. The Teec Nos Pos rug is usually quite large and is often relatively expensive.

The square Sandpainting rug, a form of Pictorial rug, is based on ceremonial sandpaintings and is thus often considered controversial, even though there is no such thing as a ceremonial rug. The background color is invariably tan or gray. Other colors of the designs are black, red, blue, and white. Hosteen Klah, a medicine man who created sandpaintings on the ground for curing ceremonies, was one of the first people to weave a Sandpainting rug.

The unbordered Crystal rug employs soft earthtones of rust, brown, gold, and gray, with occasional accents of pastels. The design incorporates bands of wavy lines alternating with solid color bands. Other design elements are squash blossoms, diamonds, stars, or geometrics.

The Pictorial rug is a reflection of the weaver's everyday life. It is a landscape that might include a hogan, a pickup truck, horses, sheep, cattle, clouds, railroad trains, flags, slogans, cartoon characters, a woman weaving at her loom, and even airplanes and helicopters. Pictorial rugs are quite accurate representations, with colors that mirror the subjects—blue skies, white sheep and clouds, green blouses, and red pickup trucks. Borders of the rugs are usually dark.

The Klagetoh rug resembles a Ganado rug in design, but it is predominantly gray in background rather than red. It has the center diamond pattern with black, red, and white designs. The borders are usually dark.

The Wide Ruins rug is one of the most finely woven banded textiles. It has a series of broad stripes in solid colors and other stripes with geometric designs. The Wide Ruins rug never has a border. The vegetal dyes, obtained from plants growing on the reservation, are in deep tones of brown, maroon, and mustard, with accents of soft pastels. Red is used rarely. A well-woven Wide Ruins rug is highly prized.

The New Lands rug is the latest development in Navajo weaving. It is a raised-outline weaving whose roots are in the Coal Mine Mesa area. The Navajo Nation purchased one million acres southeast of Sanders, Arizona, as a consequence of the Hopi-Navajo Land Dispute. Most Navajos from the Coal Mine Mesa area on the far western end of the reservation relocated to the new area. Bruce Burnham, a trader in Sanders, encouraged the development of the New Lands weaving style. The wool room in his trading post (page 37) has an incredible supply of soft-toned, vegetal-dyed wool skeins for the use of the New Lands weavers. The raised outline is produced by weaving a ridge that highlights the design figures of the softly colored background yarns. The raised ridge is woven on one side of the rug only, and the rug frequently has a Teec Nos Pos design.

The Tree of Life, a type of Pictorial rug, depicts a tree, sometimes shown growing from a Navajo wedding basket. The tree has multiple branches with many brilliantly colored birds perched on the branches as well as on the ground. The background is usually light colored to accentuate the brilliance of the birds in the foreground. The border is usually dark.

The Yei rug depicts the Yeis, the supernatural Holy People. The Yeis are the intermediaries between the Navajos and their gods. The Yeis restore health, physically and spiritually, in a properly conducted ceremony. Since there is controversy over this type of design, some weavers have a ceremony performed prior to weaving in order to insure balance and harmony in their lives. The colors are varied, and the border is dark.

The Yei-bi-chai rug is a depiction of a healing ceremony in which human masked dancers impersonate the Yeis. The dancers are usually woven in profile, and each has a woman as a partner. Included in the rug pattern are the patient, the medicine man, the lead dancer, and a clown that offers the much-needed laughter. The weavers usually use lifelike colors in the garments.

The Storm Pattern rug is elaborately designed. The middle of the rug depicts the center of the universe. The four corners have rectangles said to represent the four sacred mountains of the Navajo or the four corners of the world. Zigzag lightning elements connect the mountains to the center of the world. Other design elements are water beetles, clouds, feathers, and arrows. The background color is usually gray or white; other colors are black, brown, and red.

The Round rug first appeared in the early 1970s. It is completely circular and is woven in typical Ganado designs and colors. The late Rose Owens, a weaver of Round rugs, said that she used a wagon wheel for her loom.

The Two-Faced rug is difficult to weave. It is probably the rarest contemporary Navajo weaving. The two sides of the rug portray completely different designs and colors. Since the rug is doubled in thickness, it is often heavy and coarser in its texture than other designs. The rug is rare and expensive, and many collectors find it attractive because of its uniqueness.

The Four-in-One rug is another rare piece. It consists of four quadrants that are bordered overall. Each quadrant has a separate design. Some weavers have woven a Fifteen-in-One, a Twenty-Four-in-One, and even a Thirty-in-One. The only limitations on the number of sections that can be woven are the weaver's creativity, skill, and patience. This style is not often woven, and it is most highly prized.

Other types of rugs worthy of being noted are the saddle blankets; the Germantown and the Teec Nos Pos Eyedazzler with their brilliant colors, zigzags, and serrated diamonds; and the Sawmill rug with its beautiful, soft, rarely seen blue tones.

Some of the rugs have a spirit line woven with a different colored strand of yarn crossing the border. Many interpretations surround the spirit line. One weaver says that the spirit line lets out the good spirits so that she may weave another fine rug. Other weavers believe that the spirit line releases one's spirit, so that it is not caught in the design.

The Navajos began weaving as far back

as 1650. They borrowed upright loom-weaving techniques from their Pueblo neighbors. They wove in cotton until the early 1700s, when the Spanish introduced sheep to the Southwest. The Navajo women began to process the sheep's wool. This was the beginning of the Classic Period, which lasted until approximately 1865. During this period the weaving quality varied from coarse, thick utility blankets to extremely refined wearing blankets. Though the Navajos did not have chiefs as a status or rank, the Chief Blanket became prominent as a shoulder blanket for men and women. The blanket was square in shape, and when the four corners of the Chief Blanket were folded to meet at the center, the design was the same as when it was unfolded.

First Phase Chief Blankets characteristically have plain stripes of blue, white, black, and brown.

Second Phase Chief Blankets have plain stripes of blue, white, brown, and bayeta, with blocks of red. *Bayeta* is the Spanish name for an English manufactured cloth, baize. Baize was brought to the Southwest by the Spanish via Mexico and traded to the Navajos.

Third Phase Chief Blankets are extremely popular. A typical blanket has a terraced diamond center enclosing a cross. There is a half-diamond figure at each end and in the middle of the blanket's edge.

Fourth Phase Chief Blankets are rarely woven today. The stripes were subordinated to a series of squares against a solid background.

During the Transition Period (1865–1890)

Navajo weavers switched from making shoulder blankets to weaving floor rugs. The railroads brought many tourists to the Southwest. As a consequence, traders multiplied quickly, supplying the Navajos with commercial yarn and dyes, as well as commercial clothing and yard goods. This did away with the need for native-woven clothes. The quality of Navajo weaving declined immeasurably, but the Navajo women carried on with weaving floor rugs because the tourist market was active in its demands.

During the Rug Period (1890–1920) the quality of the weaving was still down. The women continued to weave at home, for their families depended on woven goods for income. Poor technique and design problems affected quality, and although there were still some excellent weavers at work, they were in the minority.

With the Revival Period (1920–present) came steps to improve the quality of yarn, colors, design, and weaving techniques all over the Reservation areas. Trader John Lorenzo Hubbell (later called Don Lorenzo Hubbell) of Ganado, Arizona, encouraged the weaving of "good" rugs. He was also responsible for securing special orders for very large floor coverings for the homes of his eastern contacts. Hubbell, the Fred Harvey Company, and the Hyde Exploring Expedition purchased only the best products of the loom for resale. Mediocrity was not acceptable. As a consequence, many Navajo families discovered that the art of weaving might be a key to financial success and personal gratification. Even though products from their looms were still called rugs, many ended up as wall hangings or tapestries—too fine to be laid on the floor and walked upon.

Another trader, J. B. Moore of Crystal Trading Post, had a profound influence on weaving. He sent wool to the East to be washed and carded. The thoroughly cleaned wool could be spun more evenly, and the technical aspect of weaving improved immensely. His influence made a great impact on the weaving of Two Grey Hills and Crystal rugs. Like Moore and Hubbell, traders Thomas Keam and Richard Wetherill also played important roles in the growth of Navajo weaving.

The traders of today still have a tremendous influence on the weaving styles and fineness of weaving. Bruce Burnham of R. B. Burnham Trading Post at Sanders, Arizona, and Bill Malone of Hubbell Trading Post at Ganado, Arizona, are two of the traders who have consistently encouraged the weavers to experiment and improve their weaving with new designs and colors.

Some weavers still produce wool from their own sheep. They shear the sheep, clean the wool, card it, spin it, dye it, and then weave the rug. Due to advances in technology, the weaver can now obtain commercially produced yarns and dyes from the traders. She can save many, many hours of wool preparation and devote her time to the skill of weaving beautiful patterns. Still, weaving is one of the most time-consuming of all Southwestern Indian crafts.

It is estimated that fifty percent of the rug weavers live on the reservation in hogans. Since the Navajos live in a matriarchal society, where helping family members is a strong

force, the weaver often discovers that there is very little money left after she sells a rug. Her family and relatives need money for food, car payments, and clothing. The money she obtains from the rug goes to maintaining the family. If she lived in the city away from the extended family, she could probably get ahead financially by being responsible only for her own rent, utilities, and food. That is not the case on the reservation. Everyone who lives in a matriarchal group lives on the same level in the hogans. In such a social environment the weaver cannot refuse to assist in her family's needs. This great feeling of responsibility to each other is undoubtedly one reason why the Navajos have survived throughout the centuries.

On the positive side, with the development of paved roads and the ownership of pickup trucks and cars, the weaver may visit several trading posts or galleries in nearby towns (such as Flagstaff, Gallup, or Albuquerque) and shop for the best price on her latest weaving. She can also go to art exhibits of contemporary Navajo work to see what other artists are doing. She can enter her work in competitions such as the Gallup Inter-Tribal Indian Ceremonial and Santa Fe Indian Market, where her work will be offered to collectors from all parts of the world. The weaver is finally able to attain recognition and adequate compensation for her art.

When purchasing a Navajo rug, one should check that the weave is tight and that the design is uniform and even from end to end. When the rug is opened fully, it should lie flat, free of wrinkles and curled corners. A Navajo rug is not one hundred percent perfect; it is not machine made. Small flaws should be accepted if they do not detract from the overall aesthetic quality of the rug. The rug should be smooth to the touch, without any lumping of the wool. Color should be uniform. Most importantly, the rug should be aesthetically appealing.

Navajo rugs invariably harmonize with all home decorating schemes—modern, Victorian, antique—whether they are hung or used as floor rugs. A Navajo rug is an example of Native American art and should be lovingly cared for. If a Navajo rug is placed on the floor, it should have a foam pad under it. The rug should be turned over periodically. If a rug is hung, it should be rotated frequently and should not be hung where the sun will fade the colors. A snapping action in the shaking of a rug will damage the warp and weft threads. Normal, light vacuuming of both sides should eliminate moths. A Navajo rug should never be washed. It should be sent to a dry cleaner, if necessary; however,

the rugs rarely need to be cleaned. A stored rug should always be rolled and never folded. Water spills should be blotted immediately to minimize the running of colors.

There are mixed opinions and attitudes regarding the future of Navajo weaving. Even though Navajo weaving is predominantly created by women, male weavers, such as Stanley Begay and James Joe, have made a positive contribution. One hopes that more male weavers will surface.

Some "experts" maintain that the number of weavers has declined drastically over the years. Others hold that although the quality of weaving has dramatically improved, the demand for first-rate weavings far exceeds the supply. However, there is a dilemma the potential weaver faces. Some of the younger people are learning the art of weaving. Others go into different fields when they leave school. Only time will tell which direction weaving will take as we approach the twenty-first century.

SADDLE BLANKETS FROM YEARS PAST, *clockwise from top left:*

Double with red and purple tassels, woven in 1940.

Single white with black, woven in 1960.

Single brown with gold, woven in 1880.

Single Germantown with fringe, woven in 1900.

Single with stripes, woven in the 1920s.

Single brown with gold squash symbols, woven in 1880.

Artists unknown. *Courtesy of Tanner's Indian Arts*

FROM YEARS PAST:

LEFT: Child's Wearing Blanket or Saddle Throw, woven in 1900, artist unknown.

Cluster pin with Kingman turquoise, made in 1950, artist unknown.

RIGHT: Woman's Wearing Blanket, circa 1915, artist unknown.

Cluster pin with Sleeping Beauty turquoise, made in the 1960s by J. M. Begay.

Below: Man's Wearing Blanket *(on floor),* woven in 1890, artist unknown.

Courtesy of Tanner's Indian Arts

FROM YEARS PAST:

Teec Nos Pos Eye Dazzler, 43 in. x 76 in., woven in 1974 by Gloria Yazzie. *Courtesy of Ron and Alissa Harvey*

FROM YEARS PAST:

Tree of Life with wedding baskets, 61 in. x 95 in., woven in 1974, artist unknown. All vegetal dyes, except for black, which is aniline dye. *Private collection*

Four Dontso figures (water creatures) and two corn plants with Rainbow God guarding the rug on three sides, 66 in. x 94 in., woven in 1972 by Bessie Bicenti. *Courtesy of Toh-atin Gallery*

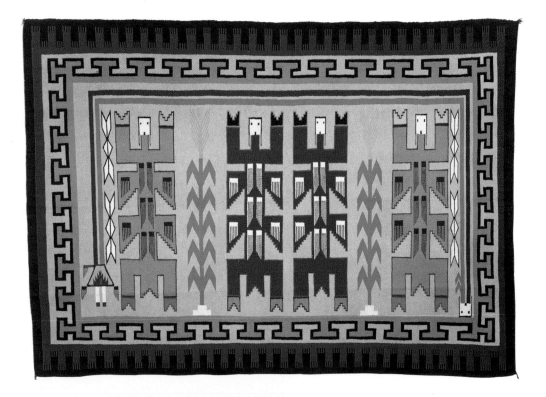

Burntwater rug, 3 ft. x 5 ft., by Cara Whitney. The displayed yarn shows the colors used in Burntwater rugs, such as the one pictured. Wool for the weaving of Burntwater rugs is processed, scoured, carded, and spun in a woolen mill. This particular yarn comes in five natural (undyed) colors such as those used for the rugs that come from the Two Grey Hills area. Aniline dyes are also treated in the mill. When the wool processing is completed, the white, light gray, and light tan skeins are given to the Navajo weavers for dyeing. The weavers gather the plants from the reservation and haul water from the windmills to boil and dye the wool, adding a mordant to set the colors. *Courtesy of R. B. Burnham & Co. Trading Post*

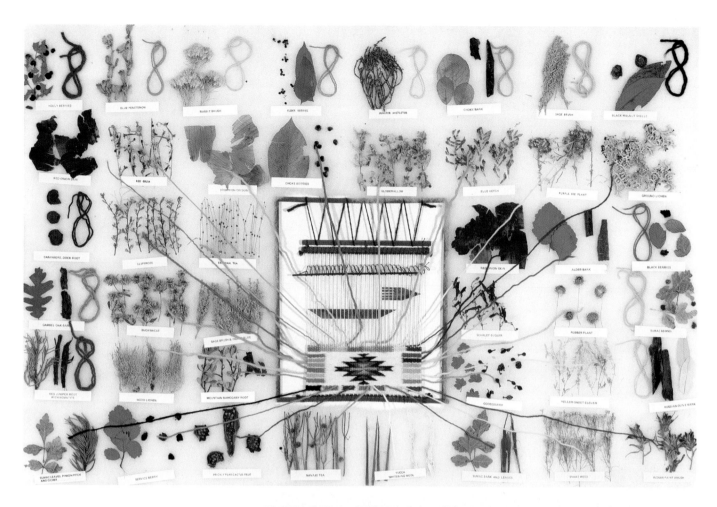

Vegetal dye display depicting the various plants that the Navajo weavers gather from the reservation to make the dyes for their rugs, by Isabell Desching. *Courtesy of R. B. Burnham & Co. Trading Post*

ALL VEGETAL-DYED RUGS:

UPPER ROW, *left to right:* Wide Ruins, 35 in. x 52½ in., by Mary C. Nez. This won Second Prize at the Gallup Inter-Tribal Indian Ceremonial in Gallup, New Mexico, in 1993.

Burntwater, 31 in. x 34¾ in., by Mary Tsinnijinnie.

LOWER ROW, *left to right:* Burntwater, 61½ in. x 95½ in., by Cara Whitney.

Burntwater, 32 in. x 52½ in., by Lorene Van Winkle.

Private collection

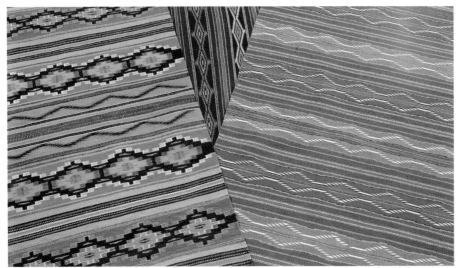

WIDE RUINS RUGS, *left to right:*

Vegetal dye, 37½ in. x 56½ in., by Elizabeth Roanhorse.

Aniline dye, 30½ in. x 51½ in., by Marilyn Roan.

Vegetal dye, 36 in. x 63 in., by Cora Gaddy.

Private collection

LEFT: New Lands raised outline, 35½ in. x 54 in., by Wanda and Stanley Begay.

RIGHT: New Lands raised outline, 46 in. x 64 in., by Jeanne Begay.

Both are vegetal-dyed rugs.

Private collection

Replica of a late 1880s
Germantown rug,
40 in. x 63½ in., by Jean
Blackhat. *Private collection*

Sawmill rug, 59 in. x 85 in., by Nonabah Harrison. This won an Honorable Mention at the Museum of Northern Arizona Navajo Show in Flagstaff, Arizona, in 1990. *Courtesy of Gary C. Newman*

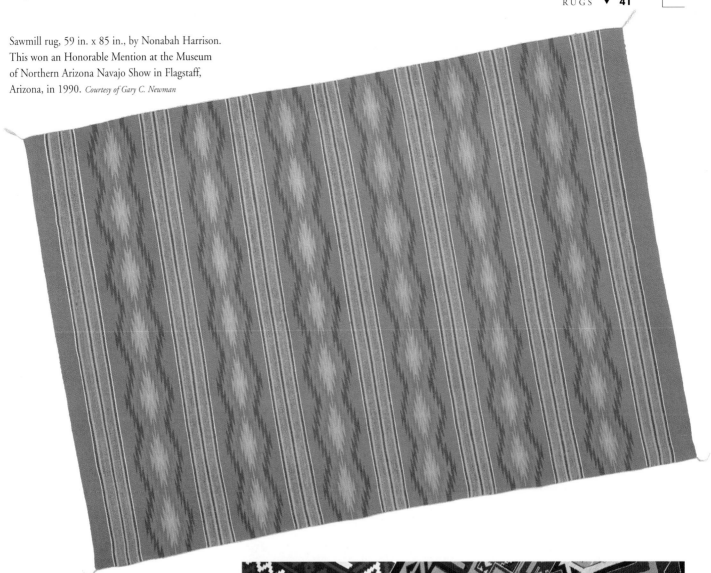

Clockwise from upper left: Chief Blanket, 46½ in. x 67 in., by Jessie Harvey.

Teec Nos Pos, 44 in. x 61 in., by Gloria Yazzie.

Ganado, 41 in. x 59 in., by Mary Shepard.

Ganado, 32½ in. x 57½ in., by Annie Yazzie.

Chief Blanket *(in corner),* 24 in. x 34 in., by Lillie Warren.

Center: Klagetoh, 48 in. x 72 in., by Shirley Joe.

Private collection

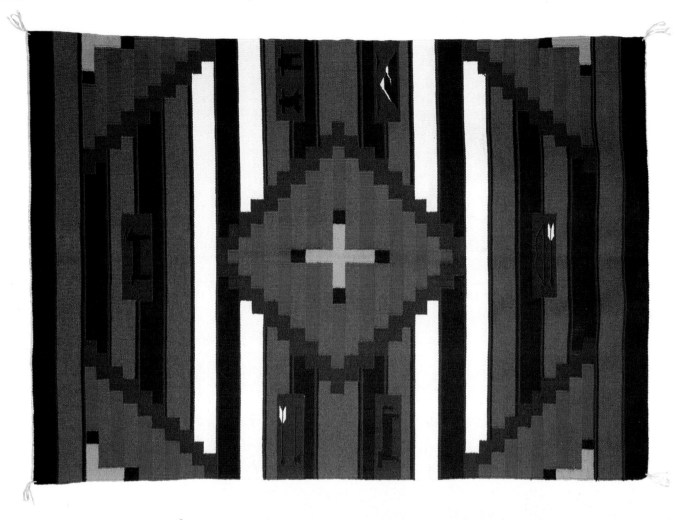

Pictorial Chief Blanket with bow and arrows, sheep, mountains, birds, and Navajo man and woman, 42 in. x 60½ in., by Eunice Joe.
Courtesy of The Kaibab Shop

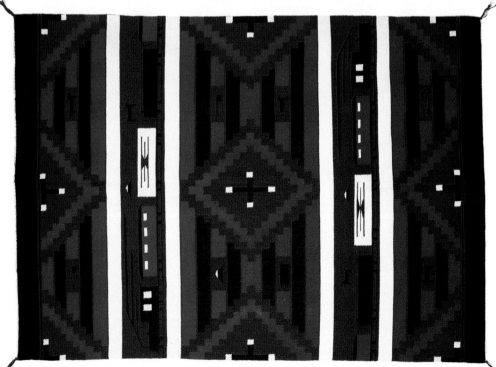

Pictorial Chief Blanket with trains, mountain, arrow, hogan (a Navajo dwelling), and sheep, 51 in. x 72 in., by James Joe. *Courtesy of The Kaibab Shop*

Rug loom with fork and spindle depicting the weaving of a Storm Pattern rug, 47 in. x 59 in., by Jean Blackhat.

Private collection

Four-in-One Storm Pattern, 47½ in. x 57½ in., by Rena Mountain. *Private collection*

THE DREAM

Over the rolling "Grey Hills" she looks,
Getting closer to her dream.
As her distance shortens, there amidst the
Blurry vision stands a man
With deep blue eyes,
Eyes so electrifying that they hypnotize.

Gazing from amongst the crowd . . .
"Is he white or is he Indian," she asks herself.
Is he really, really there or is he there by Spirit?
Will he fade into The Dream?

Taking in every breath of the Mysterious Dancers,
"Yei-bi-chais," they are the center of her dream,
So real she could almost touch the faces
of the Mysterious.

Looking out once more into the crowd,
Her mind wonders if The Dream is real
as his eyes hypnotize her,
Holding out his strong hands to hers.
He is her strength in search of that distant dream,
For there is no other Dream on the horizon,
Only the spirit that beckons.

They will create forever onward with the
    Unusual One,
For she is the Unusual One herself,
Just like The Dream.

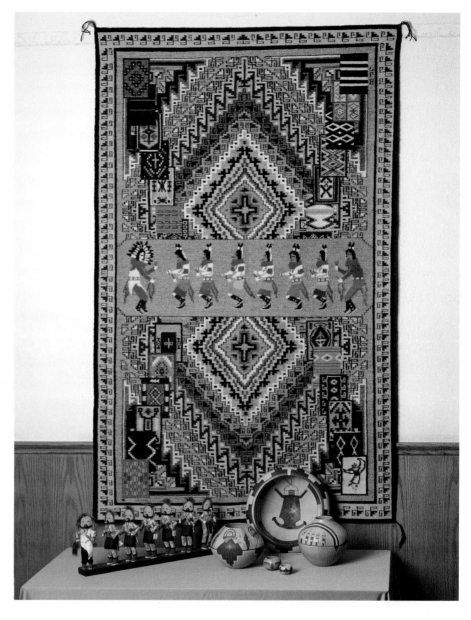

Thirty-in-One rug, 3 ft. 9 in. x 6 ft., entitled *Beyond Navajo Tradition*, by Sarah Paul Begay. The Yei-bi-chai Dancers in the center of the rug were designed by Willie Scott. Sarah worked on this rug for seven months and used seventy-one colors. The background of the rug is a Two Grey Hills design. Beginning with the left side the rugs superimposed are, *from top to bottom:* Classic, Navajo Dress, Classic, Ganado, Classic, Pine Springs, Classic, then the Yei-bi-chai Dancers. Continuing: Chinle, Classic, Burntwater, Classic, Storm Pattern, Moki, and Raised Outline. Superimposed on the right side are: Third Phase Chief Blanket, Four Corners, Classic, Teec Nos Pos, Classic Saddle Blanket, Classic, then the Yei-bi-chai Dancers. Continuing: Crystal, Old Style Crystal, Wide Ruins, Classic, Klagetoh, Classic, and Eagle Pictorial. On this page is a poem that Sarah wrote as an honor to her rug. *Courtesy of Nick Smith*

Crafts below the rug, *left to right:* Wood carved set of seven Yei-bi-chai Dancers, 7¼ in. high x 23 in. wide, artist unknown.

Pot with Yei-bi-chai Dancers, 5¾ in. high.

Miniature pot with four sacred plants design.

Miniature pot with cloud design.

Pot with Mother Earth design, 12 in. diameter x 5¼ in. high.

Pot with Yei-bi-chai Dancers and corn, 6¾ in. high.

All pots made by Ida Sahmie. *Courtesy of McGee's Beyond Native Tradition*

MY PRECIOUS CHILD
"Beyond Native Tradition"

To her loom she sits patiently
Her fingers softly whisper as she runs it through
The streams of the Warp bringing every wool to
Life, for this is her child she created.

She smiles to herself as a new design enters
her mind for she goes Beyond Native Tradition
To create for people to see, very mystic in her
own way.

For she weaves with the Universe:
    Her crosspoles made of sky and earth cords
    Her warp sticks of sun rays
    Her heddles of rock crystals and sheet lightning
    Her batten of sun halo
    Her comb of white shell and her precious golden
corn pollen at her side.

She thinks of her "Beloved Grandma" as she feels
the pride, joy, and comfort her weaving brings
to her. She gives a sigh of relief, because
she knows, she's finally there.

There she has comfort, she knows she's a
master now and whispers into Grandma's ear,
her secret. She travels on 'til the day
she will quietly put her precious tools away, which
brought her so much love, joy and comfort.

There, she will soar higher with the Universe,
for she knows her journey has ended, but her
precious Child "Beyond Native Tradition"
will soar even higher.
In her heart, she knows nobody will ever take the
child she created away from her.

Twenty-Four-in-One rug, 7 ft. x 11 ft. entitled *Beyond Native Tradition,* by Sarah Paul Begay. Sarah worked on this rug for 975 hours and used 130 colors. The outside border is a Wide Ruins design, and the inside border and background is a Burntwater design. Beginning with the left side the rugs superimposed are, from top to bottom: Raised Outline, Third Phase Chief Blanket, Four Corners, Trapezoid, Burnham, Crystal, Storm Pattern, Saddle Blanket, Two Grey Hills, Moki, and Mother Earth–Father Sky. On the right side are: Standard Style, Eye Dazzler, Chinle, Navajo Dress, Teec Nos Pos, Pine Springs, Wool Wrap Warp, Klagetoh, Yei-bi-chai, Ganado, and Bird Pictorial. The poem on this page was written by Sarah as an honor to her rug. *Courtesy of McGee's Beyond Native Tradition*

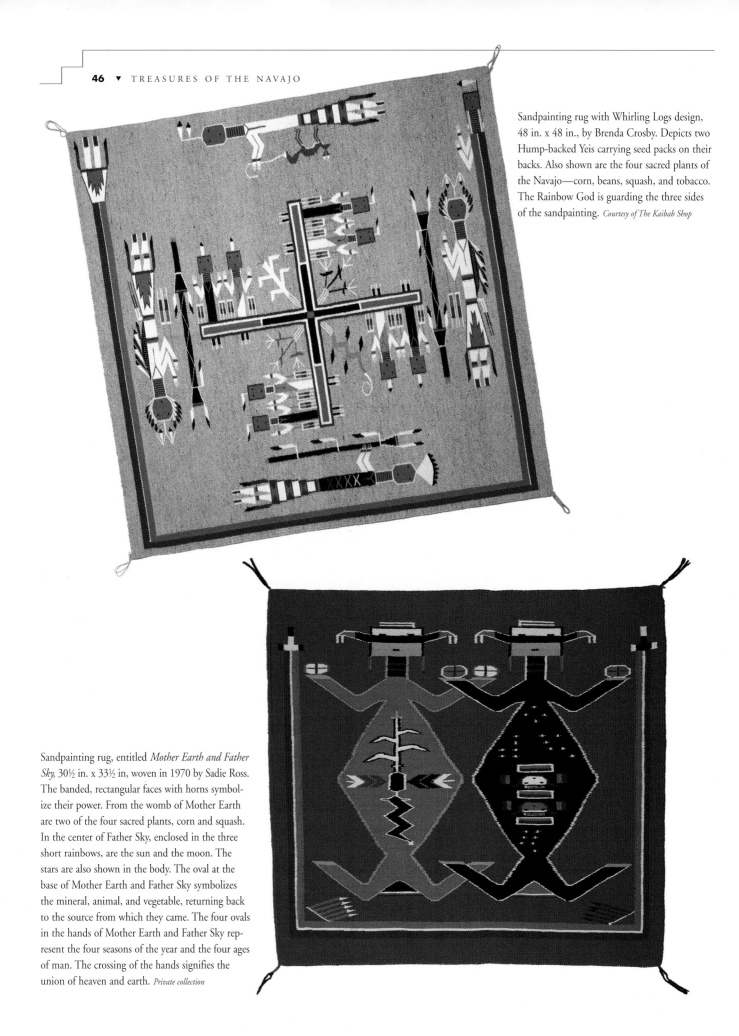

Sandpainting rug with Whirling Logs design, 48 in. x 48 in., by Brenda Crosby. Depicts two Hump-backed Yeis carrying seed packs on their backs. Also shown are the four sacred plants of the Navajo—corn, beans, squash, and tobacco. The Rainbow God is guarding the three sides of the sandpainting. *Courtesy of The Kaibab Shop*

Sandpainting rug, entitled *Mother Earth and Father Sky*, 30½ in. x 33½ in, woven in 1970 by Sadie Ross. The banded, rectangular faces with horns symbolize their power. From the womb of Mother Earth are two of the four sacred plants, corn and squash. In the center of Father Sky, enclosed in the three short rainbows, are the sun and the moon. The stars are also shown in the body. The oval at the base of Mother Earth and Father Sky symbolizes the mineral, animal, and vegetable, returning back to the source from which they came. The four ovals in the hands of Mother Earth and Father Sky represent the four seasons of the year and the four ages of man. The crossing of the hands signifies the union of heaven and earth. *Private collection*

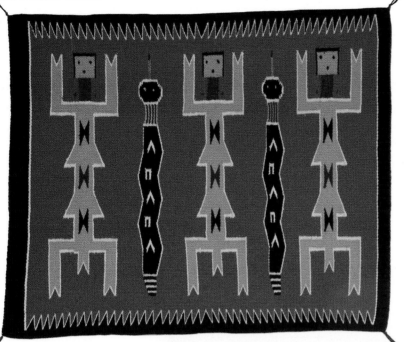

YEI RUGS, *top to bottom:*

Snake Yeis, 28 in. x 33 in., weaver unknown.
The Medicine Man had to give special permission
to the weaver in order for her to use the snake in
the weaving of the rug. *Private collection*

Hump-backed Yeis carrying seed packs on
their backs, 25½ in. x 31 in., by Ruby White.
Courtesy of Les and Pam Jensen

Corn Yeis, 22 in. x 23 in., weaver unknown.
Private collection

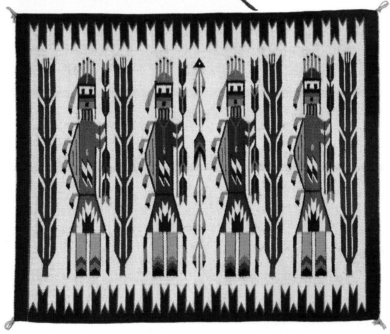

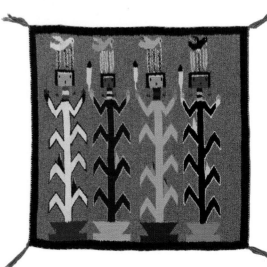

TOP: Yei-bi-chai or Fox Tail Dancers Rug, 41¾ in. x 60½ in., by Bessie Bia.

Private collection

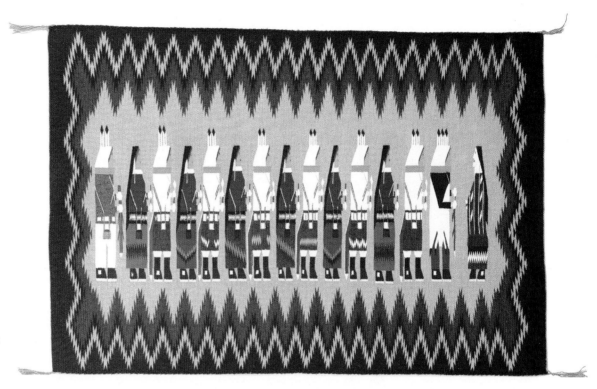

BELOW: Yei-bi-chai or Fox Tail Dancers Rug, 49½ in. x 67 in., by Louise Maloney.

Private collection

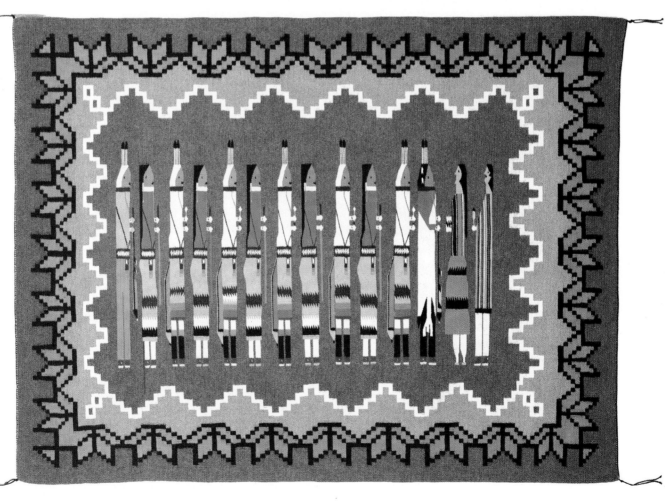

ABOVE: Pictorial rug showing the daily life-style of the Navajo, 47 in. x 61 in., by Sarah Tso. Note the lifelike figures and the rounded contours.

Courtesy of Garland's Navajo Rugs

Two-faced rug with Yei-bi-chai design, 38 in. x 46½ in., by Lucy Wilson. A Two-faced rug is twice as hard to weave as a regular rug as it requires two sets of warps and four sets of heddles. *Private collection*

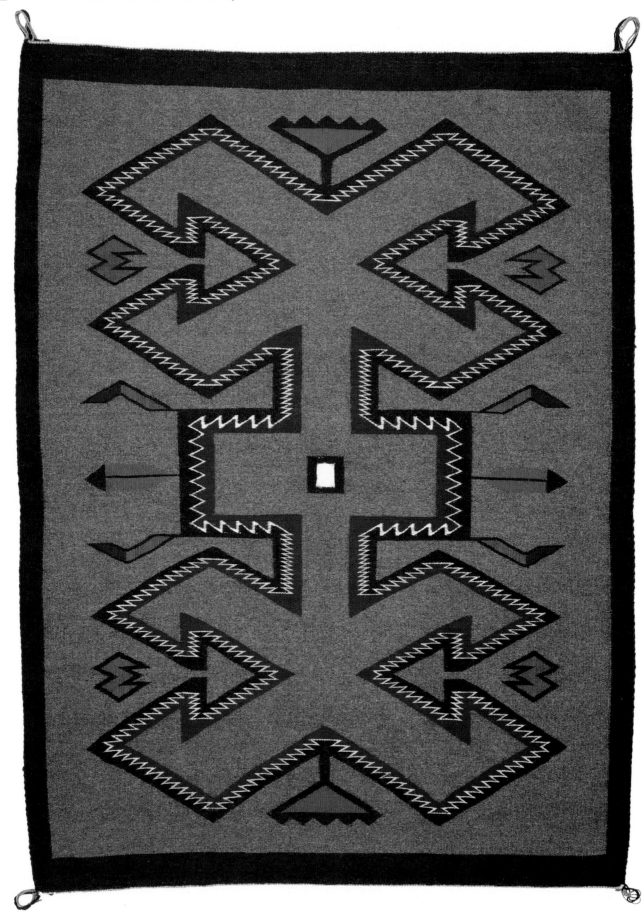

SOMETHING DIFFERENT:

Round rug with wedding basket, 36 in. diam., by Rose Owens. Rose used a wagon wheel on which to build her loom. *Courtesy of R. B. Burnham & Co. Trading Post*

Pictorial Bicentennial rug, 22 in. x 24½ in., woven in 1976 by Sadie Ross. *Private collection*

SOMETHING DIFFERENT:

OPPOSITE: Spider Woman rug, 40 in. x 53 in., by Mary Sloan. The spider comes up from a hole in the ground and offers to teach the Navajo woman how to weave this rug, which explains the hole in the center of the rug. To this day, when a girl child is born, the women in the family gather the web from the spider who has its hole in the ground and put the web on the hands and arms of the girl child to ensure that she will become a good rug weaver.

Courtesy of Ron and Alissa Harvey

PICTORIAL BIRD RUGS, *left to right:*

Thirty-four birds and seventeen blossoms on a Tree of Life, 30½ in. x 49 in., by Rena Mountain. *Courtesy of Gary C. Newman*

Seventy-two birds on a Tree of Life resting in a Navajo wedding basket, 38 in. x 58½ in., by Rena Mountain. *Private collection*

Ninety-six birds on a Tree of Life resting in a Navajo wedding basket, 37 in. x 60 in., by Jean Monroe.

Courtesy of Les and Pam Jensen

OPPOSITE: Four-in-One Pictorial bird rug with Tree of Life, entitled The Four Seasons, 44 1/2 in. x 59 in., by Bessie Sellers. The upper left quadrant depicts Spring, when the leaves are on the trees. The upper right depicts Summer, when the corn is in bloom. The lower right depicts Autumn, when the leaves have turned color. The lower left depicts Winter, when there are no leaves on the trees, and there is snow on the ground. *Private collection*

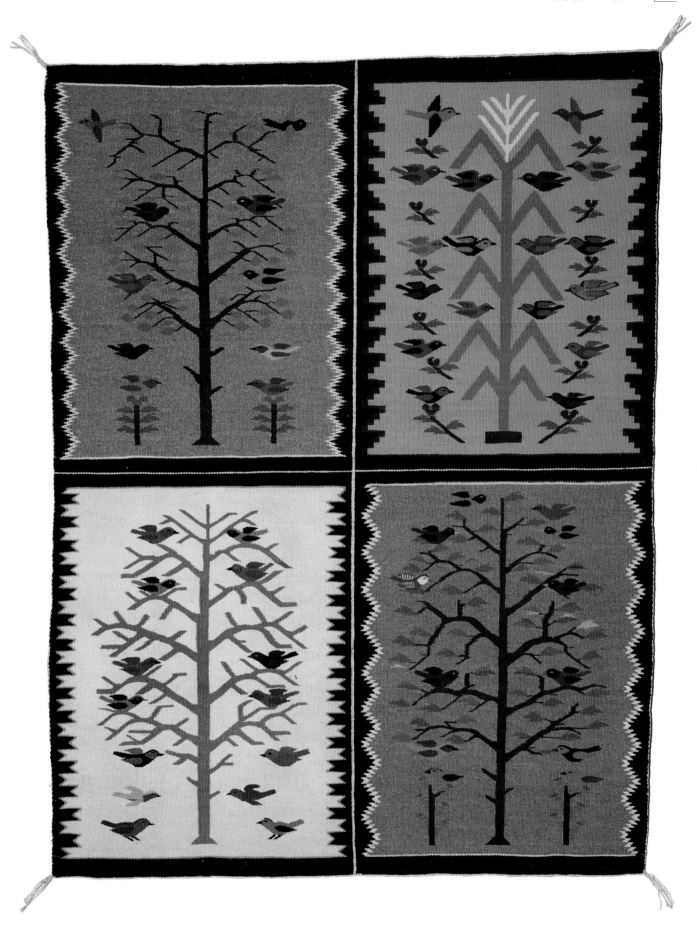

Two Grey Hills rug, 35¾ in. x 62½ in., by Mary Wadsworth. The yarn used is from all natural wool except for the black, which is an aniline dye.

Private collection

ABOVE: Fifteen-in-One rug, 45 in. x 60 in., by Minnie Yazzie. *Courtesy of The Kaibab Shop*

RIGHT: An assortment of miniature rugs from all areas of the reservation, ranging in size from 3 in. x 4 in. to 12 in. x 17 in. Weavers are Charlotte Begay, Nina Begay, Sarah Begay, Louise Bia, Rena Billie, Durwin Brown, Lula Brown, Lorraine Mark, Helen Martin, Nadine Nez, Rose Marie Nez, Lucy Roanhorse, Sarah Tisi, Darlene Yazzie, Matilda Yazzie, and Nellie Yazzie. *Courtesy of Garland's Navajo Rugs*

Sandpaintings

THE SETTING IS the Navajo hogan: Mother Earth is the floor. The entrance of the hogan faces east. The medicine man and his materials are in readiness. The patient is in place.

The purpose of this scene is the restoration of the balance of the patient's world. In the traditional Navajo world, diseases of the mind and the body arise from an interruption of *Hózhó,* the embodiment of balance, blessedness, holiness, and beauty. The patient is ill; he is not in harmony with the universe. He seeks the help of the medicine man to feel better, both physically and spiritually. The medicine man accomplishes this by means of the chant or sing, a ceremony that may last from one to nine days.

Sandpainting of a Hopi Salako Kachina, Hopi pot, Navajo wedding basket, Navajo necklace, and Zuni fetish, 20½ in. x 28 in., by James M. Cambridge. *Private collection*

The chant's purpose is to purify the patient by means of fasting, sweating, sexual abstinence, bathing, shampooing the hair in yucca suds, and a vigil. The chant invites supernatural forces to enter the ceremony through offerings of prayer sticks that contain something the gods highly cherish. Many objects have become sacred by the medicine man's acquisition of knowledge and by his performing ceremonies over them. These objects constitute the chanter's bundle. When the bundle is properly used in conjunction with songs and prayers, it will do for the patient today what it did for the deities in mythological times. The sacred objects of the bundle will help restore everything to a normal, healthful, and happy order. Once again there will be harmony and balance.

A characteristic of the chant is that in the

ceremony, or way, it is sung over a person not only to cure him of disease but also to bring blessings to him and all concerned, even to his whole tribe. Another characteristic of the chant is a lengthy song sequence that may contain several hundred songs. It is incumbent upon the medicine man and his assistants to know the songs completely and accurately in order for the chant or sing to be successful. The chant also involves the use of medicinal herbs, prayers, and sandpaintings.

A sandpainting made on the floor of the hogan by the medicine man is considered an important sacred object. It usually depicts a scene in the life of the Holy Ones. It is achieved by the sprinkling of dry sand colored with natural pigments, such as ground shell, charcoal, and pollen.

When a person sits on the unfinished sandpainting, and the medicine man (also known as a chanter) treats him by applying the sacred-bundle paraphernalia with the proper songs and prayers, he becomes the god and participates in all its supernatural powers. Often a long sequence of songs is accompanied by drumming on an inverted basket. Then a huge fire is built and the patient undergoes a sweating and ceremonial emesis. As songs are being sung, sand from the painting, along with pieces of the sacred bundle, are applied to the person's nearly nude body. When the medicine man touches a part of the figure in the sandpainting, then touches the patient with the sands, he symbolically transfers the magical potency of the sandpainting to the patient being cured. The sickness presumably falls from the patient and harmony prevails. He feels at one with the deities.

The patient signifies his acceptance of all

the gods have done for him by "breathing in" the dawn. He also understands that he must not physically touch anyone who has not been the One-Sung-Over in this chant or a similar sing because he represents a supernatural power. For that reason, he is dangerous. Harm would come to the one touched because that one is unprotected by the chant. After the completion of the medicine man's work, the patient has become the One-Sung-Over, and as such has bathed himself ceremonially in yucca suds. Now he may assume his normal position in his family. However, he is more than normal, for at different times in the chant he has been one or another of the gods.

After the ceremonial sandpainting is completed, all the sands are picked up from the floor of the hogan and placed in a cloth or blanket. The sands are removed to a place away from the hogan and scattered to the winds.

There are probably more than a thousand ceremonial sandpaintings, though less than half are produced today. In a Navajo population of over two hundred thousand, there are only about seven hundred medicine men and women. Most of these are fifty years or older. Only one or two Navajos are initiated each year. Not many of the younger people are interested in becoming chanters. As a consequence, many ceremonial ground sandpaintings are becoming faint memories.

However, in 1949 David Villaseñor, an artist from Sonora, Mexico, became interested in trying to preserve those sandpaintings in danger of becoming extinct. He developed the How-To-Do-Sandpainting Kit—and in 1972 he and Jean Villaseñor wrote a very well illustrated book entitled *How To Do Permanent Sandpainting*. This was a great step in the making of permanent sandpaintings on boards.

The sandpainter collects rocks on the Navajo reservation. He obtains red from sandstone, yellow from ocher, black from charcoal, blue from a mixture of gypsum and charcoal, white from pulverized gypsum, and turquoise. The sandpainter uses cornmeal, crushed flower petals, and pollen. The rock is hammered and broken up into small pieces, which the sandpainter allows to dry. Then he grinds and pulverizes the pieces by using a mortar and pestle or a kitchen meat grinder. After grinding, the sand is sifted and strained into several grades of fineness.

Sheets of plywood or particle board—three-eighths or one-half inch thick—are sawed into the sizes and shapes desired. The edges are sanded smooth. The sandpainter spreads glue evenly over the entire surface and places the boards in the sun to dry further.

Before the actual painting begins, he determines which ceremony he wants to do: the Storm Pattern, Yei-bi-chai and Yei Whirling Logs, Hump-backed Yeis with Feather Maiden, or Hump-backed Yeis with the Four Sacred Plants. Or he may decide to do non-ceremonial subject matter such as a Hopi Salako and Hopi pot, a peyote rattle and fan with a turquoise necklace, or a wedding basket and wedding vase. The menu is varied and unlimited. The artist sets his own sights; he allows his flights of fancy to soar.

The sandpainting of the pot, bear fetish, and hump-backed flute players (see frontispiece) by Eugene Baatsoslanii Joe exemplifies a uniqueness of style and excellence of design. Baatsoslanii is descended from a long line of medicine men. He is an outstanding artist who has won numerous awards for his gifted work.

The sandpainter uses fine brushes to outline the design in glue. He does one section at a time so that the glue does not dry before he applies the sand. He also uses one color of sand at a time to prevent the overlapping of colors. Before the second color and second section is begun, he waits until the first section has thoroughly dried. Then he places a small amount of sand in his palm just under the second finger. He allows the sand to trickle out from the index finger, regulating the flow with his thumb. The flow is usually gentle, soft, and even, to insure straightness and clarity of line. The most skilled sandpainter works entirely by eye.

When the sandpainting is completed, it is set out to dry for a couple days. Then the entire surface is sprayed with a fine mist of shellac. This coating insures that the sand granules do not fall off. Any loose sand particles are softly brushed away.

Even though there was much criticism of the sandpainters who worked on boards with glue, the production continued. The criticism that disharmony would occur did not frighten off the painters. They were more angry that their right to individual choice was at issue than the likelihood their actions would cause unbalance and disharmony. No sandpainters would admit they were endangering themselves or their tribe.

Yet, in works for sale, some Navajo artists made subtle changes in the true details of the ceremonials. These changes, they hoped, would avoid offending the Holy People. In addition, the board sandpaintings became ceremonially inaccurate, useless, and therefore harmless. The conflict between the medicine man and the artist narrowed a little.

A few Navajo artists have combined oil or acrylic with the sands. The effects have been stunning. Bobby Johnson was one such artist who created lovely work, painting pottery and landscapes. In 1987 he won nine awards in the Gallup Inter-Tribal Indian Ceremonial. Tragically, later in the same year, at the age of twenty-eight, he was killed in an automobile accident.

Artists like these have made the Navajos world leaders in the art form of sandpainting. Sandpaintings are one of the least expensive handcrafted art forms and one of the few with deep cultural significance. The prices run the gamut to suit all budgets—from souvenirs in gift shops to museum-quality collectibles in galleries.

Sandpaintings make excellent wall hangings. They are very durable and require little care. An occasional feather dusting is all that is needed.

When purchasing a sandpainting, look for precise lines and colors that blend well. The intricacy of the design must please the eye. The sandpainting must be viewed as a fine work of art. It is maintained that one picture in sand is worth a thousand words, especially to a culture that until recent decades did not have a written language.

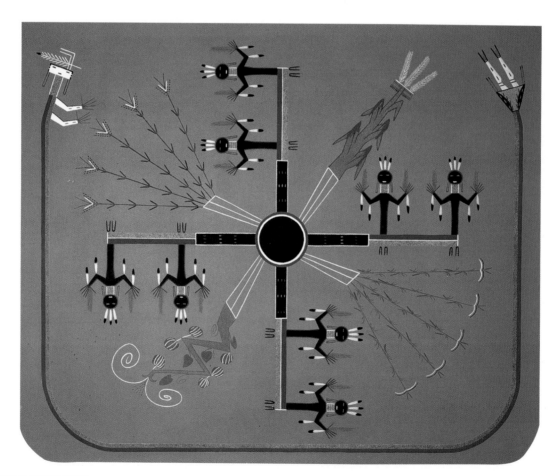

FROM YEARS PAST:

Whirling Logs sandpainting, 39 in. x 48 in., made in 1970 by Alfred Watchman. The four sacred plants of the Navajo, corn, beans, squash, and tobacco stretch their roots into the black circle of water, where the four logs trapped at the confluence of the male and female rivers whirl around the center. The seated Gods complete the design. The Rainbow Goddess with a shooting chant face and head feather guards the three sides of the sandpainting. Private collection

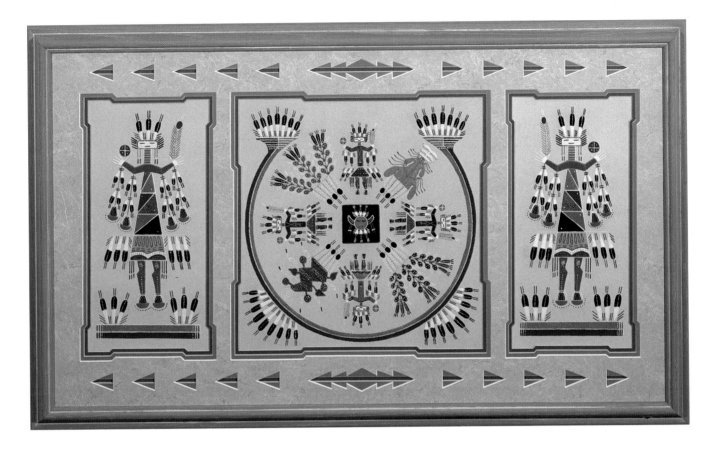

ABOVE, *left and right:* Sandpaintings, 6 in. x 12 in., depict Yei figures each holding a basket in one hand and a prayer feather in the other. Short rainbows are at the base of the Yei figures.

Center: Sandpainting, 12 in. x 12 in., depicts the sun (in center of painting), which represents protection. The buffalo horns are the symbol of strength, and the eagle feathers at their tips represent balance and justice. Circling the sandpainting is a rainbow garland with magpie feathers. The corn, beans, squash, and tobacco are the four sacred plants of the Navajo. The four Yei figures hold a basket in one hand and a prayer feather in the other.

Made by Rosabelle Ben. *Courtesy of McGee's Beyond Native Tradition*

LEFT: Sand and acrylic painting, 18 in. x 18 in., by Bobby Johnson. *Private collection*

Sandpainting of four Hump-backed Yeis with mountain sheep horns, 16 in. x 16 in., by Johnny Benally, Sr. They are the Gods of Harvest and have deerskin bags on their backs to hold the seeds for planting. Eagle feathers are on the back of the bags. The corn, beans, squash, and tobacco are the four sacred plants of the Navajo. The four Little Summer Thunders have rain falling from their outstretched arms. Four mountains guard the opening of the sandpainting, and the rainbow garland circles three sides. *Courtesy of McGee's Beyond Native Tradition*

Sandpainting of two Hump-backed Yeis with mountain sheep horns, 12 in. x 12 in., by Bernice Bahe and Rosie Yellowhair. The Hump-backed Yeis are the Gods of Harvest and have deerskin bags on their backs to hold the seeds for planting. Each holds a basket in one hand and a medicine bag in the shape of a weasel in the other. The Feather Maiden in the center has the corn and lightning in her body. *Courtesy of McGee's Beyond Native Tradition*

TOP: Sandpainting of Yei and Yei-bi-chai Whirling Logs, 15½ in. x 15½ in., by Diane Thomas. The rainbow garland and feathers circle the sandpainting, with mountains guarding the opening.

Courtesy of McGee's Beyond Native Tradition

BOTTOM: Sandpaintings of Hopi Kachina Dancers, each 5½ in. x 11½ in., by Albert Yazzie. Kachinas are, left to right: Mountain Lion Kachina, Early Morning Kachina, Early Morning Kachina, Deer Kachina.

Courtesy of McGee's Beyond Native Tradition

Sandpainting of peyote rattle and fan, Navajo neck-lace, wedding basket, wedding vase, Santa Clara pot, and Zuni fetish, 24 in. x 24 in., by Samuel Cambridge. *Private collection*

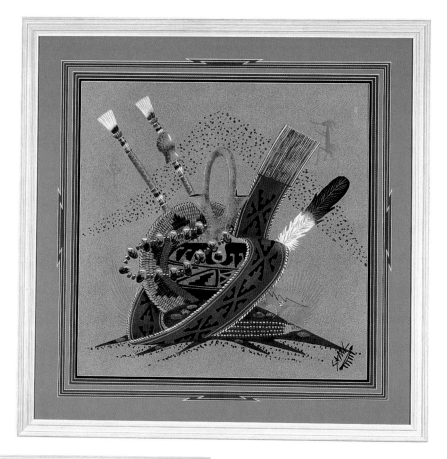

Sandpainting depicting the sky world, 24 in. x 24 in., by Wilford Rotsinah. White represents the dawn; blue, the sky; yellow, the sunset; and black, the night sky. The Little Summer Thunders in the dawn, day sky, and sunset, hold out their arms with the falling rain. The stars and constellations are in the night sky. The corn, beans, squash, and tobacco are the four sacred plants of the Navajo. Blue and gray bats are guarding the openings, and the rainbow garland completely encloses the sandpainting. *Private collection*

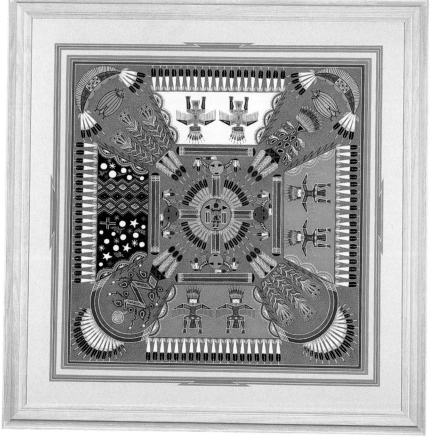

OPPOSITE: Sandpainting of pot and bear fetish, 14 in. x 16 in., by Eugene Baatsoslanii Joe.

Flutes, by Jerry Nells.

Fetishes, by Tony Lee.

All courtesy of Many Hands Gallery

Paintings

IN INDIAN SOCIETY everyone participates in art to some extent. Painting is strange to no one. Painting is not set aside to view only on special occasions and holidays as in a museum, but is extremely integrated with everyday life. Modern Navajo painting is a way of sharing beauty as well as a philosophy of life. Navajo paintings are modern in spirit. They invariably represent the evolution of the Navajos' own traditions. Navajo paintings are unique, and in no way are they borrowed from the Anglo artist.

The concept of easel painting, an Anglo-European technique, was completely unfamiliar to Native Americans prior to the

RIGHT: *Songs From Red Canyon,* acrylic, 40 in. x 50 in., by Tony Abeyta. The Yei-bi-chai Dancers are people impersonating the Yeis, deities of the Navajo, in sacred Navajo dances. *Private collection*

twentieth century. The Native Americans painted on a flat horizontal surface.

Easel painting was introduced in the 1930s by Dorothy Dunn, a trained artist. Her efforts convinced United States government officials that painting classes would benefit talented Indian students. She was a teacher at the government-sponsored Santa Fe Indian School, which was interested largely in the culture of the Southwestern Indian tribes. Her objectives were to stimulate the appreciation of Indian painting among the students and the general public, to maintain the tribal and individual differences in painting, to explore traditional Indian art methods, and to encourage new styles, motifs, and techniques in harmony with the old. Her primary aim was that the students discover in easel art a medium to create unique images that reflected their cultural heritage.

In the fall of 1932 the Studio—as Miss Dunn's painting and design classes were called—began on an experimental basis. It was a momentous occasion, marking the first formal advancement of painting by Southwestern Indians.

Even though abstract art was the rage of the international art market, Miss Dunn insisted on emphasizing and encouraging the traditional art style of the Southwestern Indians. It was this influence that predominated the Studio teachings. Miss Dunn taught at the Studio for five years. After this short period of time, Gerónima Cruz Montoya, a San Juan Pueblo artist, became the principal director of the Studio for twenty-five years. For thirty years Miss Dunn's basic methods and philosophy flourished with no significant changes. Almost all of the important Indian painters of her generation came under her guidance or were taught by her students. These painters, in turn, taught most Indian artists of the succeeding generation. The legacy she handed down had the effect of a pebble dropped in a pond of water and creating patterns of concentric circles.

Jim Abeita was born in 1960 in Crownpoint, New Mexico. He is a Navajo artist who paints whatever he sees easily and naturally. His paintings have a magical quality. His ability to paint people, horses, and action is remarkable. His detail is accurate and meticulously depicted. Abeita's painting reflects realism, action, and excellent perspective.

Narciso Abeyta, also known as Ha-So-De, was born in 1918 in Canyon Chico, New Mexico. Abeyta was never concerned with minute detail, but only with the sweep and dash of movement in wild, free scenes. In his painting *Chicken Pull,* three men mounted on powerfully proportioned horses are painted in browns, with soft reds providing relief. Their mission is to race to the chicken, which has been buried in dirt with only its head sticking out, and to pull it out of the ground. When this is accomplished, each person tries to get a piece of the chicken.

Ha-So-De studied under Dorothy Dunn in the Santa Fe Indian School. Later he became a teacher at the Studio. His themes are traditional, bold, individualistic. He paints about his land, his people, and native culture. The scenes are exotic in feel and quality. Some critics liken his work to the French nineteenth-century painters Henri Rousseau and Paul Gauguin. Abeyta's work is widely collected in this country, Europe, and Japan.

Navajo painter Tony Abeyta was taught by his father, Ha-So-De. Other influences on his early development were Earl Biss, Dan Namingha, Allan Houser, Fritz Scholder, and the school of contemporary Indian painters. Tony studied art in France and Italy as well as at the Institute of American Indian Art in Santa Fe, the Maryland Institute of Fine Arts, and the Art Institute of Chicago.

Abeyta says, "I was born in 1966 and raised in Gallup, New Mexico, amidst the Navajo, Zuni, and surrounding reservations. I work predominantly with traditional themes and imagery, although I wasn't raised in a traditional atmosphere per se. I focus on the religious and spiritual aspects of Native American culture, for these have been the basis of the culture's strength and endurance. Within this context I have grown and learned some of the essential values which exist in Native American society. To work in the rest of the world with its foreign complexities is truly a challenge. To create purely, intuitively, and honestly and to evolve the process of art is always a struggle for all artisans. This is my primary focus, currently and for years to come." Tony uses bright, intense colors. He loves being a painter, and he creates approximately ninety paintings a year. He has opened his own gallery in Taos, New Mexico.

Harrison Begay was born in 1917 in White Cone, Arizona. He enrolled in the Santa Fe Indian School and attended Dorothy Dunn's art classes when he was sixteen years old. His work as a student was quite remarkable. His focus was on the landscape, the red rocks and cliffs, the mountains.

Begay has been a full-time artist since 1947, gaining worldwide recognition and acclaim. His subjects are scenes from everyday Navajo life—dancers, children at play, sheepherding, and training horses. He also paints scenes inspired by the Navajo understanding of the creation of the four sacred mountains.

One of his popular themes is a Navajo girl and her sheep. This scene evokes charm, delicacy, and quietness as the girl holds a lamb in her arms, flanked by a sheep on either side. The shepherdess is serene. His painting *Torch to Start the Squaw Dance* shows a rider on horseback carrying the prayer sticks from the dance just ending and delivering them to the next dance about to begin.

Begay notes that the subjects of most of his paintings are of the present, everyday tribal life. He has done some legendary and ceremonial painting due to his great interest in sandpaintings, which he considers examples of the most highly developed paintings of his own tribe. He feels his tribal art is well worth preserving and that Indian art ought to be characterized by the styles and effects his forefathers developed.

Harrison Begay is undoubtedly the best known of the Navajo traditionalist artists. His output is voluminous. Despite the acclaim and honors he has received, Begay maintains that he knows nothing about art—he just knows how to paint. Be that as it may, anyone who owns a Harrison Begay has a treasure.

Tony Begay was born in 1941 in Ganado, Arizona. He painted Navajo subjects realistically—the people, their landscapes, and their art. Begay was proficient in all the media in which he painted. His brushwork was clean and his colors, rich. He was equally at home in oil, acrylic, watercolor, pen and ink, and pastel.

The late 1960s and 1970s was a time of social unrest and protest. Militant Indian organizations, such as AIM (American Indian Movement) influenced contemporary Indian art. Tony Begay responded to this part of native culture with stunning and dramatic paintings.

Begay died in 1973 in a tragic accident. He was not only respected for his artwork but was also popular with his peers. Though he died at an early age, his legacy was momentous.

James Cody lives in Tuba City, Arizona, and is about fifty years old. Some thought he was a most promising Navajo painter, but his interest in painting waned, and he gave up his career in order to become a minister. He is a born-again Christian and is involved in the revival circuit.

Robert Draper was born in 1938 of a Navajo mother and a Hopi-Laguna father. His beautiful and colorful landscapes of mesas and canyons are widely acclaimed. Though he paints in oil, acrylic, and pastel, it is as a watercolorist that he is most ingenious. Over the years his colors have become deeper and more varied and his technique more precise. In the late 1960s and early 1970s his subject matter included prehistoric pictographs, conquistadors, abstractions, and historical depictions, such as *The Long Walk,* which he painted during the centennial year commemorating the return of the Navajos from captivity in New Mexico to their homeland. Eventually he found a niche that satisfied him—the landscapes of the Navajo reservation.

W. B. (Bill) Franklin was born in 1947 at Ganado, Arizona. He has been a full-time painter since 1986. Franklin has painted in a variety of styles and seems to have found gratification in his rug design compositions. He has used oil, acrylic, watercolor, pen and ink, pencil, pastel, stone, silver, gemstone, and print as media. Franklin is certainly talented enough to make a meaningful contribution to Navajo art.

R. C. Gorman, born in 1932 in Chinle, Arizona, is probably the most widely known Navajo artist. He is outgoing, outspoken, flamboyant, thoughtful, and controversial. He is a disciple of the Dorothy Dunn Santa Fe Indian School philosophy. He thinks she made an indelible and everlasting contribution to the shaping and forming of Indian painters by giving them a start. However, this did not prevent him from using the traditional art teachings to catapult into the avant-garde world of painting. It was in 1958 that the Navajo tribe gave him a scholarship to attend Mexico City College. The exposure to the artwork of Siquieros, Orozco, and Rivera was mind-boggling to Gorman.

Gorman excels in the media of drawing and painting. His work exudes form, power, and beauty. He simplifies by omitting non-essentials and by strongly accenting essentials.

Thematically, his work focuses on the Indian, whether it be Navajo rugs, Yei-bi-chai masks, traditional pottery motifs, or the Long Walk tragedy, which he poignantly featured in some of his 1968 paintings.

However, it is Gorman's drawings and paintings of Navajo women that evoke universal appeal and recognition. When a sophisticated art enthusiast or a relatively new art viewer see his Navajo women on canvas and exclaim, "That's a Gorman!" the artist could receive no greater accolade.

Tony Hood is a resident of Church Rock, New Mexico. He paints only in watercolors, but also does pen-and-ink sketches. His artwork provides him with supplemental income. He is a counselor at various Bureau of Indian Affairs (BIA) boarding schools.

Raymond Judge was born in 1945 in Lower Greasewood, near Ganado, Arizona. He is the son of Rose, a weaver, and Slim Judge, council leader and medicine man. Raymond lives in Flagstaff, Arizona, and is a part-time painter. He likes to paint animals and birds. His media are watercolor, tempera, acrylic, gouache, pencil, pen and ink, pastel, and prints.

James King was born in 1951 in Shiprock, New Mexico. He was educated at the University of Utah. In 1980 he won the Triple Crown of Indian Art—Best of Show at the Gallup Inter-Tribal Indian Ceremonial, Best in Oil at the New Mexico State Fair, and Best in Oil at the Santa Fe Indian Market. He is extremely encouraging to Navajo young people who wish to pursue their artistic talents. The State of New Mexico commissioned King to create a large painting, now hanging in the rotunda of the Capitol Building in Santa Fe, New Mexico. He works in the media of oil, acrylic, watercolor, pencil, pastel, stone, and prints.

Jerry Lee was born in 1944 in Wide Ruins, Arizona. His favored themes are hunters, horses, and fawns. The red cliffs he likes to paint bring out his effective pastel colors in a dramatic way. Lee has been a student of Harrison Begay and Beatien Yazz. His media are watercolor and acrylic.

Redwing T. Nez was born in 1960 in Winslow, Arizona. He paints in the three-dimensional European style. His subject matter favors animals and landscapes.

Occasionally he does abstracts. He uses bold colors and paints in oil, acrylic, watercolor, and mixed media.

Quincy Tahoma (1920–1956) developed his own style. He was a traditional painter whose art reflected the Navajo's love of homeland and a kinship with animals, both wild and domestic, including horses, antelopes, deer, and bear cubs. His pictures portrayed impressions of Navajo life and ceremonies with much dynamic action and sometimes whimsy. Whatever Tahoma did, he did well. His draftsmanship was clean, and his colors were harmonious and rich.

From its beginnings, Navajo art emphasized storytelling. Tahoma carried storytelling one step further with his signature, which was part of a miniature scene, painted in black silhouette within a yellow semicircular backdrop. This little vignette described the action that was to take place after the action in the completed painting. Tahoma chose to tell two stories and also to reveal his humor as an artist. Unfortunately, Tahoma, who experienced adversity most of his life, died at the age of thirty-five.

Calvin Toddy was born in 1955. He is a son of Jimmy Toddy, Sr. (Beatien Yazz). He achieves unusual results when he uses watercolor as a media. His pieces capture the moment; his perspective is unerring. In his snow background paintings, one can feel the cold. Toddy enjoys painting the Navajos as they carry on their everyday activities. He has a special love for depicting their breathtaking landscapes. Toddy works in the media of oil, acrylic, watercolor, silver, and gemstone.

Irving Toddy was born in 1951. He,

too, is a son of Jimmy Toddy, Sr. Irving works as a Navajo tribal administrator. He is a prolific painter and his work is diverse and experimental. He is noted for portraiture, and his groups of Navajos wearing their weavings are amazing. His media include oil, acrylic, watercolor, pencil, pen and ink, conté crayon, charcoal, and film.

Bruce Watchman is in his forties and lives in Window Rock, Arizona. Though not a full-time artist, he is widely known for his figures and portraits. His medium is watercolor.

Tom W. Yazzie is a famed Navajo wood carver. His dolls of gods that participate in Navajo ceremonies are a complement to the painted versions by Bruce Watchman and Tony Hood. Yazzie is now a retired bus driver who paints in his spare time, though he prefers to carve. The dolls he continues to make do not end up in the conventional retail stores and galleries, as he has a large collector base and private following.

Beatien Yazz (Jimmy Toddy, Sr.) was born in 1928 near Wide Ruins, Arizona. He illustrated two popular novels written by Alberta Hannum in the 1950s, titled *Spin a Silver Dollar* and *Paint the Wind.* They became classics of Southwestern literature. The books were a fictionalized account of Yazz's experiences.

When Yazz was eight years old, he was drawing with crayons at the Wide Ruins Trading Post, operated by Sallie and Bill Lippincott. He drew pictures of small desert creatures and of ceremonial figures on every scrap of paper he could find. The Lippincotts

recognized and encouraged his talents.

Yazz later went to the Indian Art School in Santa Fe, New Mexico. He encountered personal difficulty in balancing Anglo and Indian cultures but he persevered. His composition is good, and his work is original. His colors are strong and bold, rarely muted. Together, Yazz and Harrison Begay are probably the most prolific of the traditionalist painters. Yazz's media include oil, acrylic, casein, tempera, and watercolor. His three oldest sons, Calvin, Marvin, and Irving, are painters, and three of his other children—Frances Toddy, Jimmy Toddy, Jr., and Orland Toddy—have also entered the field of art.

In recent years, Yazz's eyesight has deteriorated. His glaucoma is no longer treatable, and he has only peripheral vision. He continues to paint, but only in a limited fashion. Fortunately, the art world has benefited from his huge repertoire of magnificent paintings, which proudly endures.

The artists mentioned above are but a few of the many Navajo painters worthy of recognition. Their work demonstrates that even though Indian art is old, it is alive, dynamic, and modern. Even though the artwork has a primitiveness, it also has a sophistication and subtlety. Indian art is both classic and modern at the same time. In addition, Indian painting will undoubtedly become more understood and appreciated as America allows itself to awaken and become aware of its indigenous cultural riches.

FROM YEARS PAST:

The Weaver, oil, 18 in. x 24 in., painted
in 1962 by Tony Begay.
Courtesy of Martin Link

FROM YEARS PAST:

Mother and Child, mixed media,
23 in. x 25 in., painted in 1970
by Beatien Yazz. *Private collection*

FROM YEARS PAST:

Chicken Pull, watercolor, 23 in. x 30 in., painted in 1973 by Ha-So-De (Narciso Abeyta). *Courtesy of Martin Link*

GODS FROM NAVAJO CEREMONIES, *left to right:*

Child-Born-of-the-Water, watercolor, by Bruce Watchman.

Fringe Mouth, watercolor, by Tony Hood.

Talking God, watercolor, by Bruce Watchman.

Paintings are 8½ in. x 11½ in. Corresponding dolls carved from cottonwood root, 12 in. high, were made by Tom W. Yazzie from 1965 to 1967. *Courtesy of Martin Link*

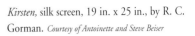

Kirsten, silk screen, 19 in. x 25 in., by R. C. Gorman. *Courtesy of Antoinette and Steve Beiser*

Left to right: Tending the Flock, watercolor, 16 in. x 17 in., by Harrison Begay. *Courtesy of Tanner's Indian Arts*

Torch to Start the Squaw Dance, watercolor, 17 in. x 19 in., by Harrison Begay. *Courtesy of Tanner's Indian Arts*

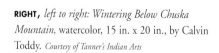

ABOVE: *Dusk,* silk screen, 19 in. x 24 in., by R. C. Gorman. *Courtesy of Antoinette and Steve Beiser*

RIGHT, *left to right: Wintering Below Chuska Mountain,* watercolor, 15 in. x 20 in., by Calvin Toddy. *Courtesy of Tanner's Indian Arts*

Today's Journey, watercolor, 15 in. x 19 in., painted in 1949 by Quincy Tahoma.

Courtesy of Tanner's Indian Arts

Evening Stroll, oil, 16 in. x 20 in., by Irving Toddy. *Courtesy of Puchteca*

Evening Herd, oil, 20 in. x 30 in., by Redwing T. Nez. *Courtesy of Antoinette and Steve Beiser*

Midnight Whistle, acrylic, 22 in. x 30 in.,
by W. B. (Bill) Franklin. *Courtesy of Puchteca*

FAR LEFT: *Weavers Image,* oil, 11 in. x 14 in.,
by Jimmie Abeita. *Courtesy of Tanner's Indian Arts*

LEFT: *Man with Bola Tie and Earring,* oil, 16 in. x
20 in., by Jimmie Abeita. The model for the painting was Preston Scott. *Courtesy of Tanner's Indian Arts*

ABOVE: *Awaiting a Storm,* watercolor, 10½ in. x 16 in.,by Robert Draper. *Courtesy of Puchteca*

RIGHT: *The Hunters,* gouache, 11 in. x 15 in., by Raymond Judge. *Courtesy of Puchteca*

The Dreamer, acrylic, 13 in. x 15 in., by Jerry Lee.
Courtesy of Puchteca

Sacred Circle, oil and acrylic,
24 in. x 35 in., by Irving J. Toddy.

Courtesy of Tanner's Indian Arts

ABOVE: *The Blessing of Shiprock,* oil, 24 in. x 36 in., by James King. *Courtesy of Tanner's Indian Arts*

Moonlit Night, oil, 24 in. x 30 in., by James Cody.
Courtesy of Martin Link

OPPOSITE: *Rio Grande Waterfowl*, oil painting with sand, 50 in. x 70 in., by Tony Abeyta. The birds are all pottery motifs from the Northern New Mexico pueblos and from the Hopi Pueblo in Northern Arizona. *Courtesy of the artist*

ABOVE: *Mother Earth, Father Sky Contemplating the Science of Spirituality,* oil painting with sand, 60 in. x 110 in., by Tony Abeyta. The sun, moon, stars, and constellations are in the body of Father Sky. The Milky Way is represented by the zigzag line which stretches from wrist to wrist. The four sacred plants of the Navajo—corn, beans, squash, and tobacco—are emanating from the womb of Mother Earth. *Courtesy of Ernest and Edith Schwartz*

Baskets

EARLY NAVAJO BASKETRY was limited in scope and was rather crude in appearance. Baskets were woven in the shape of water bottles and carrying baskets. The water bottles were quite simple and undecorated. They usually had long necks and a round base, twelve to sixteen inches in diameter. They were made in a coiled weave, and the stitch counts were low. The majority of water bottle baskets had three or four stitches to the inch, while the number of coils ranged from three to four per inch. All in all, a rather loose arrangement. The first carrying baskets were wicker with loose weaving and unfinished edges. They were used to gather and carry plants, yucca, and cactus fruit.

The Navajos also made different water jar baskets, which had handles, usually two per jar, and were also loose in weave. Water jar baskets are still made today in far fewer numbers, even though they are superior in terms of tightness of weave and in the decorative quality of the horsehair handles.

These forms were coated inside and out with pinyon pitch or resin to make them watertight. The pitching also served the

The wedding baskets inside the trunk date from 1980 to 1993, artists unknown.

The wedding baskets on the floor date from 1860 to 1920, artists unknown.

Transitional Moki reproduction rug *(on wall)*, 56 in. x 72 in., by Jennie Slick.

J. B. Moore rug *(on floor)*, 42 in. x 61 in., woven in 1920, artist unknown.

Courtesy of R. B. Burnham & Co. Trading Post

purpose of covering up the poor quality of the sewing in the older pieces.

From 1868 to early years of the twentieth century the Navajos made shallow baskets for ceremonial rites, utilitarian purposes, and for holding small objects. From 1920 to 1970 the baskets were used only for ceremonials. From 1970 to the present, the baskets found a ready and eager commercial market in the non-Navajo world. These baskets were generically known as wedding baskets.

The Navajo wedding basket, one of the most recognized Southwestern Indian baskets, has been woven by the Navajos, the Paiutes, the Apaches, and the Utes. In the nineteenth century there was a shift from Navajo-made to Paiute-made wedding baskets. Navajo women weavers were subjected to so many restrictions that they stopped making wedding baskets.

These are but a few of the taboos: No one could watch a woman weave a basket. The work had to be done some distance away from the hogan. A woman could not work on a basket if she were menstruating. No one could touch a woman while she was making a basket. Blood must never touch a ceremonial basket. A weaver could not sleep with her husband while making a basket. If a man should make a basket (a small number of men do weave baskets today) he would become impotent. A woman must have a sing over her both before and after starting the basket. Some Navajo singers told the women they would become ill if they wove baskets at all. With all these restrictions, it is no small wonder that the number of basketmakers and baskets made declined

so drastically among the Navajo women. It wasn't until the 1960s that the Navajo women resisted that kind of thinking and began to reject and ignore the taboos.

The Navajo wedding basket is woven with sumac, used for the warp, and dyed mountain mahogany, for the weft. Occasionally sumac is used for both warp and weft. The wedding basket is a coiled basket, stitched over a three-rod triangular foundation. The rim is finished in a herringbone weave. The basketmaker uses dyed elements to create the design, choosing among the basic colors of white, natural, red, reddish brown, and black. In more recent years aniline dyes have been introduced, providing brighter tones of red and orange.

The women gather the sumac in early spring and the mountain mahogany in winter. The preparation of the materials follows. This involves peeling, splitting, twisting and braiding, soaking, and coloring. The materials are soaked in warm water for fifteen minutes before the coiling begins. This soaking makes the materials pliable, so they are easier to handle, speeding up the time in which a basket can be constructed.

The basketmaker takes a prepared piece of sumac, pushes the sharpened sewing end through a center hole made with an awl, then loops around and back into the center hole. This sewing action is continued until a full circle, the center spot or core, is completed. Each stitch should be next to the previous one. The basketmaker continues to make holes with an awl, pulling the sumac through each hole to the left of the stitch in the previous row. A medium-grade Navajo wedding basket will have nine to ten stitches to the inch. A very high quality basket will be woven fifteen to eighteen stitches per inch. The Paiute women, mainly on the western edge of the Navajo reservation, are famed for their tightly coiled baskets, and they make baskets the year round. They have succeeded at selling to the trading posts, where their baskets are bought by Navajos and tourists.

The wedding basket contains much symbolism and much interpretation. Triangular designs represent hills and valleys of this world and the underworld. The spirit line break in the circular design reflects the communication between the two worlds. As a consequence, spirits are free to come and go between the two worlds. The center spot or core of the basket denotes the emergence of the Holy People—First Man and First Woman—into the present world, known as the Fourth or Glittering World. Earth is the area surrounding the core. The first layer of black triangular design represents the four sacred mountains, the boundaries of Navajo lands. The area adjacent to the black design symbolizes the sky, and the red design depicts clouds and darkness. The white in the basket represents the dawn.

Designs are geometrical shapes and tiered block patterns, always with a path of exit or spirit line, a narrow strip where the design does not quite meet. The Navajos believe that a completed circle will imprison the spirit and creativity of the maker. The terminal end of the rim coil is always directly above the spirit line. In ceremonies, when the basket is full, the medicine man knows where the spirit line is by finding the end of the rim with his fingers. Then he orients the basket so that the spirit line will always face east.

Navajo lore indicates the Navajo basket is sacred and filled with power. The Navajo wedding basket plays a commanding role in ceremonial rites. It has probably been in many sings and filled with cornmeal and pollen, or used for the ritual bath, or turned upside down and beaten with the palm of the hand as a drum. When used as a drum, the wedding basket is a focal point in one of the most important Navajo rituals, the Night Dance.

Although the wedding basket has many usages, folklore tells us the use of the basket in the wedding ceremony is the origin of the name "wedding basket." When a Navajo man and woman decide to get married, the Navajo bride-to-be cooks cornmeal in three colors—red for health, blue for happiness, and white for wealth. During the marriage ritual, the medicine man places the wedding basket with the cooked meal between the couple. The bride washes her groom's hands in a water-filled bowl; then he washes her hands. The bride takes a pinch of the cornmeal from the east side of the basket; the groom does the same. After this is eaten she takes cornmeal from the south, west, and north sides; the groom mirrors her each time. Then together they take meal from the center of the basket to eat. The ceremonial basket is then passed around to all of the guests, who take a pinch until the basket is empty. After the meal is eaten, the groom's mother removes the basket, which is not seen the rest of the evening. She puts it away—never to use it again. But Navajo folklore also tells us that it can be used for a *Kinaaldá* (a girl's puberty rite) and then return it. In another account of the passing of the baskets among the guests, the guest who eats the last pinch of cornmeal receives the wedding basket.

Most of the time these baskets are given or sold to the trading post for safekeeping. Depending on what the Navajo wishes, the trader will not sell the baskets but will keep them until they are required for the next ceremony. The baskets, however, may be used and resold many times. It is not unusual to buy a Navajo wedding basket and find the residue of cornmeal in its stitches. In fact, a trading post on the Navajo reservation might report that approximately three hundred Navajo wedding baskets, all for Indian use, will come into and go out of the trading post in a year's time. This does not mean that three hundred new baskets are woven. Rather, it shows that the same baskets are in and out of the trading post a number of times, as "repeats." One trader estimates that perhaps only one out of every twenty or thirty baskets is new.

Basketmakers are now creating different design motifs, such as butterflies, coyotes, Yei and human figures, as well as the old designs. They employ a full range of colors by using aniline and vegetal dyes and make very large baskets in addition to excellent miniatures. The new basketmakers have gained acceptance in the marketplace. Collectors have found their works in trading posts in the Southwest. Galleries and museums have also accepted the new wave of basketry. Navajo basketmakers are able to earn substantial income from their artistry. In spite of all the changes, the basketmaker must still be a botanist, a colorist, a weaver, a designer, and a poet—all in one.

A good basketweaver usually has a keen sense of symmetry, balance, and proportion. She also incorporates her designs and colors with artistic taste. A finished basket is truly awesome considering the lack of precision instruments (only an awl is used) and the reliance on the eye. The quality of coiled baskets is high today, though this has not always been the case. The basketmaking craft almost dropped out of sight, mainly because of the many taboos imposed on the weavers who made baskets.

Selecting a basket to buy is a highly personal matter. Each single element should be of consistent size and color. The design should be well placed on the basket and in the correct proportion to the size of the basket. Repetitive designs should be evenly spaced. As is true in any purchase of a work of art, buy it because you like it and because you believe it is fairly priced for your needs.

Once you have made the purchase, you may want to display it so that you and others will enjoy it. Keep your basket clean. Do not display it in kitchen areas—grease and dirt are not kind to a basket. Avoid direct sunlight on the basket. Also avoid areas of excessive moisture or excessive dryness. Check the basket occasionally for insect damage. Vacuum it with a soft brush. Handle the basket carefully to avoid damage. Always use two hands to pick up the basket—one to guide it, the other to balance it. A good basket deserves loving care.

WEDDING BASKETS, ABOVE, *clockwise from top right:* Butterflies, 23½ in. diameter, by Corena Fuller. *Private collection*

Rain and cloud design, 17 in. diameter, and 6 in. deep, weaver unknown. *Courtesy of Steve and Mary Anne Sewell*

Rain and cloud design, 16¾ in. diameter, by Betty Fuller. *Private collection*

Cloud and rain design, 21¾ in. diameter, by Kathy Bryant. *Courtesy of Les and Pam Jensen*

Cloud and rain design, 15½ in. diameter, by Corena Fuller. *Private collection*

Cloud and rain design, 19 in. diameter, weaver unknown. *Courtesy of Steve and Mary Anne Sewell*

Basket with eagle in center and butterflies around the edge, 30 in. diameter, by Nora Endichy. *Courtesy of Les and Pam Jensen*

RIGHT: The making of a Navajo wedding basket, by Mary Secody. The material used is sumac. *Private collection*

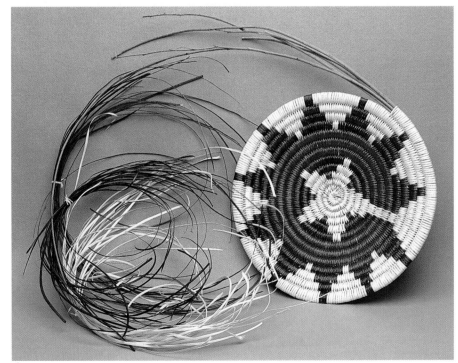

Treasures Unlimited

WHEN ONE THINKS of Navajo arts, one invariably visualizes rugs, jewelry, sandpaintings, pottery, paintings, and baskets. However, other creative areas also demonstrate the versatility of the Navajo artist. Many of these are illustrated in the photographs that follow.

In recent years some Navajos have made beadwork an important part of their creative output. Navajo beadwork expresses a deep-rooted spirituality in its patterns of light and color. The beadworkers strive to create beauty from the resources of nature and from within themselves.

FROM YEARS PAST:

Eight Navajo cloth dolls dressed in velvet, made in the 1950s, artist unknown. *Courtesy of Tanner's Indian Arts*

The cloth dolls of clowns made by Shilene Morris always bring on a smile. They radiate whimsy and humor, as do the eight Navajo cloth dolls sitting so regally on a highchair, decked out in colorful velvet dresses, adorned with necklaces and sequins.

On a more serious note, the dolls made by Kay Bennett celebrate the young girl entering womanhood in the Navajo puberty ceremony, the Kinaaldá. The dolls are quite elaborate. The boy's shirt and girl's blouse are in traditional velveteen. The boy wears cotton trousers and the girl, a full satin skirt. Details include beads for the necklaces, rings, bracelets, and silver buttons sewn to the blouse. The smiles on their faces indicates that all is well with their world.

The Navajo cradleboard is an everyday object that can also be beautiful. It has two boards tied together at the center and double pointed at the top, with a thin sheet of wood that is bent for the hood of the cradle. Cloth is used for padding, sides, and ties. At the bottom of the cradleboard is a wooden footrest.

The woodcarving of Tom W. Yazzie illustrates three silversmiths at work, each one using a different technique in the making of a bracelet. Yazzie uses poster paint to emphasize what has already been carved. He tends to use a different color for each shirt in a given group.

Leslie Nez constructed a scene made of wood depicting everyday Navajo life. This typical vignette features a hogan, a woman grinding corn, a wood fire with a coffeepot and teapot, and the ever-present dog and sheep.

One may not think of saddle making as an art, but the superb large saddle made by Jake Livingston shows excellent workmanship and unmatched artistry. His saddles are as much in demand as is his jewelry. This many-faceted artist is very well known for his jewelry, but his versatility knows no bounds. After observing Hopis making clay figures, he decided to experiment in clay, which subsequently led to the making of bronze sculptures. He made several bronze figures that fit into the category of Western art, and then went on to create a sculpture of a Navajo woman adorned in a squash blossom necklace, silver buttons, and turquoise earrings.

The 1980s ushered in a sudden increase of sculpture in the world of Indian art. Navajo artists began to work in alabaster and in bronze. The number of artists expanded dramatically, the market scene was favorable, and the quality of the art was high.

Sculptor Garry Geneeha attended the American Indian Arts School in Santa Fe, New Mexico. He took a class in sculpture, bought a piece of alabaster, and sold it immediately after it was carved. The sculpture is now in the Navajo Nation Museum as part of its permanent collection. Garry says that he feels lost when he is not working, as he enjoys his work immensely. What began as an interest in making money has evolved into something sacred and a spiritual outlet. He feels that the alabasters are like his children and that Mother Earth blessed him with the alabaster and her goodness. Before he starts to work he says prayers, makes offerings of corn pollen, and burns cedar. When he sculpts he sings songs, and his good feelings come out to make his sculptures good. He belongs to the Native American Church and also to the Mormon Church. He says that it's a paradox trying to take the best from both worlds.

One of his sculptures of Utah alabaster is a poignant scene of father and son doing a gourd dance. The other sculpture shown here is of an older Navajo woman holding a Navajo rug draped over her left arm and offering a compassionate peace gesture with her right hand. The simplicity is dramatic.

Tim Washburn's alabaster sculpture of a woman holding a Navajo rug shows a dignified woman sharing and showing her rug with pride. Randall Beyale's alabaster sculpture of a woman dancing displays a freedom of movement in her face and in the flaring of her skirt.

Tomas Dougi, Jr., was born in Kaibeto, Arizona, in 1948. He was a recognized sculptor whose spiritual visions came alive in many colors of stone. He developed a distinctive style that led him to fame. Dougi enjoyed working in Carrara marble, quarried in Italy, even though marble is the most difficult stone to sculpt. His repertoire included ceremonies, memories, relationships, and women whose faces were influenced by his mother, Ceclone Smallcanyon. Dougi's work is exhibited in museums throughout the world. His work has tremendous power and appeal. His hope that it would occupy a significant niche in the art of sculpture has been fulfilled. Tomas Dougi died in Flagstaff, Arizona, at the age of forty-six.

Larry Yazzie was born in 1958. He began sculpting in 1985, using alabaster, marble, and steatite. Then he began to create bronzes. At first his pieces were small, but he soon discovered that bronze collectors wanted large pieces. Some of his pieces are larger than life-size and are dramatic and powerful. He states that his bronzes represent all of the Indian people and that his work is strongly connected to his spirituality. He likes what he accomplishes and respects what he is doing. He emphasizes quality of work rather than quantity. He feels that if he is to survive as an artist, he must pace himself because the work is strenuous. He describes himself as having been a workaholic and says that

he had to slow down when the work became too stressful. He realized then that his first priority had to be his family. His work is distinguished by its clean lines and a gracefulness of movement.

Various artists make sterling silver eating utensils, pillboxes, teapots, or baby rattles. The possibilities for artistic expression are limitless. Still other artisans make ceramic Yei-bi-chai masks, chairs and chair cushions, pitch baskets, fuzzy sheep and goats, belt looms and belts.

Elizabeth Abeyta was exposed to art from the day she was born. She is the daughter of the painter Narciso Abeyta (Ha-so-de). Her mother, Sylvia Ann, has always worked in clay. Since clay was readily available around the house, all the children made clay figures. Elizabeth always felt that she was at one with the earth. As a young child she would take off her clothes and play in the mud, earning the affectionate nickname Toadie.

Even as a youngster she knew she would become an artist. She made a living from her charming clay sculptures when she was still in her twenties. In 1974 she studied at the Navajo Community College, and from 1976 to 1979 she studied three-dimensional design and sculpture at the Institute of American Indian Arts in Santa Fe, New Mexico. In 1980 she won a scholarship to the San Francisco Art Institute for one year.

Elizabeth's sculptures are varied—some whimsical, some elegant, and some filled with spiritual meaning. She loves her work. Often she doesn't realize how wonderful her sculpture is until it is finished. Then she stands back, looks at it in awe and says, "Did I do that?"

She loves people and exudes warmth. She finds that friendships are wonderful and amazing happenings. She feels that people have something inside of them that is missing, and when we meet other people and form friendships, that missing piece fills up.

The following photographs are illustrations of Navajo technical skill in "arts and crafts." These skills demonstrate the flair the Navajos have for translating their artistic leanings into new and exciting adventures. This is how art survives; it is also how art grows.

FROM YEARS PAST:

Navajo scene with hogan, horse, bench with tortillas, wood fire with coffeepot and teapot, dog, sheep, wood pile, unattended rug-weaving loom, summerhouse, water barrel, sweat lodge, and woman grinding corn. Made in the 1970s by Leslie Nez.

Courtesy of Tanner's Indian Arts

FROM YEARS PAST:

Left to right: A silversmith uses the stamping technique in the making of a silver bracelet. The bracelet has an old green Cerillos turquoise stone from the 1930s.

A silversmith uses the hammering technique in the making of a silver bracelet. The bracelet has nine #11 Arizona mixed turquoise stones made in 1940.

A silversmith uses the sand-cast technique in the making of a silver bracelet. To the right of the figure is part of the tufa mold in which the silver is poured, and the unpolished silver is resting against the mold. The bracelet has a Lone Mountain turquoise stone and won Second Place at the New Mexico State Fair in Albuquerque, New Mexico, in 1974.

All of the figures were made in the 1960s by Tom W. Yazzie. The bracelets are by unknown artists.

All courtesy of Tanner's Indian Arts

LEFT: These sheep and goat figures are constructed on a wood frame and then covered with the hide and wool of sheep and goats. Sizes range from 10 in. to 28 in., artist unknown. *Courtesy of Emerald Tanner*

Large saddle *(at top)*, by Jake Livingston. A dollar bill was placed under the padded seat during construction so that whoever is riding on the saddle would never be broke.

Rope and quirt, made in the 1920s, artist unknown.

Saddlebags, by Mike Tsosie.

Double saddle blanket with stripes, 31 in. x 62 in., by Shirley Tsinnie.

Ganado rug *(left)*, 41 in. x 61 in., by Bah Yazzie Ashley.

Traditional saddle in foreground, made in 1900, artist unknown. The ceremonial buckskin under the saddle is used in Navajo ceremonies and sometimes by a sandpainter for his ritual sandpainting.

All courtesy of R. B. Burnham & Co. Trading Post, except saddle and buckskin, courtesy of Bill Malone

Ceramic mask of Yei-bi-chai Dancer, 13 in. x 13 in., excluding feathers.

Male figure *(left)*, 18 in. high, and female figure *(right)*, 15 in. high, are from the Yei-bi-chai group.

Made by A. Dempsey. *Courtesy of Tanner's Indian Arts*

Chair, by Joe Aragon.

Chair cushions, by Sadie Kanuho.

Cradleboard, made in 1947 by Kescoli Benally the First for his granddaughter, Virginia Burnham, on the day she was born.

Small pitch basket with horsehair handles *(left)*, 10 in. high, by Bessie Owl.

Large pitch basket with horsehair handles, 16 in. high, by Bessie Holiday. This won First Place at the O'odham Tash Show in Casa Grande, Arizona, in 1991.

Courtesy of R. B. Burnham & Co. Trading Post

Navajo dress, by Felicia Nez. The dress was woven on an upright loom, as were the rugs.

Belt, made in 1960 by Marie Joe.

Pin with Lone Mountain Spider Web turquoise stones, from dead pawn, made in 1930, artist unknown.

Squash blossom necklace, from dead pawn, made in 1970 by Roanhorse.

Silver buttons, made in the 1930s by Kescoli Benally the First.

Two Grey Hills rug (left), 24 in. x 34 in., by Mary L. Ben.

Transitional period revival rug (center), 39 in. x 58 in., by Jolene Tsinnie.

Double saddle blanket (right), 31 in. x 61 in., by Bessie Yazzie.

Wedding baskets, artists unknown.
All courtesy of R. B. Burnham & Co. Trading Post

Tall basket, 10½ in. x 23⅝ in., made by Anna Mae Jim. *Courtesy of Garland's Indian Jewelry*

Cloth dolls of clowns, by Shilene Morris.

Turquoise and red belts, artist unknown.

Courtesy of McGee's Beyond Native Tradition

SILVER WORK:

Clockwise from top: Two-handled bowl; thimble with turquoise stone; salt and pepper shakers, by Jeffrey Castillo; baby spoon, by Jeffrey Castillo; baby rattle; teapot with turquoise stone; wedding vase; pill box; milk can with turquoise stone.

Center: Spoon and fork set, by Thomas Curtis.

Unless otherwise noted, all made by unknown artists. *Courtesy of McGee's Beyond Native Tradition*

ALL STERLING SILVER:

Teapot with two cups and one spoon, by Charley Spencer.

Bottle, 9¾ in. high, by Nelson Emerson.

Kachina figure, 9¼ in. high, by Nelson Emerson.

All turquoise is Kingman turquoise. *Courtesy of Gallup Indian Plaza*

BEADWORK:

Bottle, by Leanne Bluehorse.

Moccasins, from dead pawn, artist unknown.

Purse, by Elsie K. Morgan.

Belt buckle and long earrings, by Marie Gleason.

Necklace, by Laura Yellowhair.

Key holder, pen holder, and hoop earrings, artists unknown.

Courtesy of R. B. Burnham & Co. Trading Post

Naf-bah, bronze sculpture of a Navajo woman wearing a squash blossom necklace with a Kingman turquoise stone and three sterling silver buttons, 18 in. high x 10 in. wide, by Jake Livingston, #1 of 20. *Courtesy of Judy Johnsen*

Dolls, 27 in. high, by Kay Bennett, depict the Kinaaldá Ceremony, the coming of age ceremony for the Navajo girl. *Courtesy of the artist*

The miniature rugs at the base of the dolls were made by Susie Bia, Nellie Tsosie, and Elizabeth Begay. *Courtesy of Tanner's Indian Arts*

In the Kinaaldá, the male figure is her partner and is usually her first beau. When the Ceremony has been completed the Medicine Man says this prayer for her:

> *In Beauty you walk,*
> *Beauty about you . . .*
> *Beauty below you . . .*
> *Beauty all around you . . .*
> *In Beauty you walk.*
> *You are now a young lady, you are now*
> *   responsible for your relatives.*
> *Be wise all your life for you and your family.*
> *You can take part in all the Ceremony.*
> *   You can carry the sacred stick.*

THREE UTAH ALABASTER SCULPTURES,
left to right:

Memory, 16 in. high.

Remembrance of a Past Love Song, 22½ in. high.

A Midnight Prayer, 16 in. high.

All made by Tomas Dougi, Jr.

Courtesy of McGee's Beyond Native Tradition

Alabaster sculpture of a woman holding a rug, 20 in. high, by Tim Washburn.

Alabaster sculpture of a woman dancing, 16½ in. high, by Randall Beyale.

Courtesy of Kay Bennett

TWO UTAH ALABASTER SCULPTURES,

left to right:

Like Father Like Son: Gourd Dancers, 25½ in. high.

Peace Offering, 26 in. high.

Both made by Garry Geneeha.

Courtesy of McGee's Beyond Native Tradition

Ceramic sculpture of Mud Head Clowns, pottery vessels, snakes, and leaves entitled After the Rain, 19 in. high x 15 in. wide, by Elizabeth Abeyta. The sculpture symbolizes the male rain. The Mud Head depicts the earth, mesas, and plateaus. After the rain has fallen, the landscape colors become intense and rich. The rain, just as the sunlight, is necessary for survival. "The vessels at the base of the Mud Heads portray the people we are," Elizabeth said. The flow of the rain accentuates the vibrancy and joy of being alive. *Courtesy of Many Hands Gallery*

Invocation, bronze sculpture of a Navajo woman, 11½ in. high x 19 in. wide, by Larry Yazzie, #3 of 24. This won First Prize at the Museum of Northern Arizona Navajo Show in Flagstaff, Arizona, in 1990. *Courtesy of Judy Johnsen*

GLOSSARY

▼▼▼

ANILINE DYE A commercially prepared chem-ical dye used in basketry and rugs to produce bright colors.

APPLIQU In jewelry, any ornamentation that is soldered to the silver base, such as leaves or flowers. In pottery, the addition of clay to the exterior of a pot in order to create a design.

BATTEN A flat wooden tool used in weav-ing textiles to keep the shed open while a weft is inserted. The shed is an opening between front and back warps.

BAYETA The Spanish name for baize, a deep red woolen cloth the Navajo weavers unraveled to make yarn in the past.

BEZEL A thin silver band that holds a stone in place and anchors it to the main part of the jewelry.

BOSQUE REDONDO The area near Fort Sumner, New Mexico where the Navajos were interned by the United States govern-ment 1863–1868. *See* Long Walk.

BOW GUARD A wide leather band worn on the wrist, formerly used to protect the wrist from the snapping of the string when using a bow and arrow. Now it is used as an ornament. Also called *ketoh* or *gato.*

CARVING Removing part of the clay from the pot to create a geometric design or a scene such as recessed cliff dwellings.

CASTING Pouring molten metal into a mold, which is removed when the metal has hardened.

CHIEF BLANKET A shoulder blanket

shaped so that the longer dimension runs from side to side rather than from top to bottom.

CHIEF BLANKET, FIRST PHASE Features plain stripes of blue, white, black, and brown. The dark blue stripes are in the center, and the end stripes are black.

CHIEF BLANKET, SECOND PHASE Features plain stripes of blue, white, black, and bayeta, with short red bars set into each blue stripe in the end and center.

CHIEF BLANKET, THIRD PHASE Features a terraced diamond center enclosing a cross, with a half-diamond figure at each end and in the middle of the blanket's edge.

CONCHA A round or oval disk stamped with designs and/or set with stones.

CONCHA BELT A group of conchas joined together to create a belt.

DEAD PAWN Pawn that is not redeemed after the agreed time. *See* Pawn.

DIN The Navajo people.

DRUM POT A drum created by stretching a piece of hide over the mouth of a ceramic pot to create a resonant sound when beaten with the palm of the hand.

ENEMY WAY A three-day curing cere-mony conducted in summer months only. Also called Entah.

ENTAH *See* Enemy Way.

FILIGREE The use of scrolls of fine wire to produce delicate, lacelike ornamentation in jewelry.

GATO *See* Bow guard.

GERMANTOWN YARN A commercial American yarn colored by chemical dyes, originally manufactured in Germantown, Pennsylvania.

HEDDLE Part of a textile loom used to control a set of warps.

HOGAN A six- or eight-sided traditional Navajo dwelling.

H ZH The embodiment of balance, blessedness, holiness, and beauty.

INCISING Drawing a pointed stick through the wet clay surface of a pot to create an accent of shallow lines.

KINAALD A Navajo girl's puberty rites.

KETOH *See* Bow guard.

LONG WALK A four-hundred-mile walk forced on the Navajos in 1863 and 1864 by the United States government and supervised by the Army. It began in Fort Defiance, Arizona, and ended at Bosque Redondo, adjacent to Fort Sumner, New Mexico, where the Navajo prisoners were interned for four years.

LOOM A wooden frame used to stretch warps for weaving a belt or rug. Navajo looms are set upright on the ground.

MANTA A shawl or cape that is wider than it is long.

METATE A grinding stone.

MODELING Adding or attaching decora-tive elements to a pot by scraping to-gether or mounding the clay from the walls of the pot.

MOKI DESIGN A simple, striped, historic

blanket design. In the 1870s this design became bold, terraced, and serrated. Moki is also a term formerly used for the Hopi Indians.

MORDANT An element in dye that sets the color.

NAJA A crescent-shaped pendant.

NEEDLEPOINT Stones that are pointed at each end, then set in a silver bezel.

NIGHT CHANT OR NIGHT WAY A major curing ceremony that takes place over nine days during winter, also known as a Yei-bi-chai Dance because dancers are costumed to impersonate the Yeis.

PATHWAY A narrow, light-colored band running from the center to the edge of a basket, or through the border of a rug. Also known as a spirit path or spirit line.

PAWN Jewelry or other items given as security for money or goods borrowed from a trader. *See also* Dead Pawn.

PETITPOINT Stones that are rounded on one end and pointed at the other, then set in a silver bezel.

PITCH A boiled pine sap used on the exterior of Navajo water-bearing baskets.

PLAITING A basketweaving technique in which the wefts and warps are similarly flat and thin. Both elements are active, crossing over and under each other.

RAISED OUTLINE A rug-making technique in which diagonal lines are highlighted by the use of additional weft strands.

REPOUSS A jewelry-making technique in which a design is created by hammering from the underside.

SADDLE BLANKET A small blanket designed for use under a horse's saddle, usually woven in a thick handspun twill.

SANDPAINTING A curing ceremonial picture made on the ground with colored sands by a medicine man. Also, a painting done on board using colored sands and glue.

SING A ceremony performed by a medicine man to restore a person's health. Also called a chant or way.

SPIRIT LINE A line extending from the background to the outer edge of a rug, created with a contrasting color of wool. *See* also Pathway.

SQUASH BLOSSOM NECKLACE A necklace of silver beads with pomegranate-like silver pendants and a naja hanging from the center.

SQUAW DANCE The non-Navajo name describing the Entah or Enemy Way ceremony.

STAMPWORK Hitting a stamp or punch with a hammer to impress a pattern in silver.

TAPESTRY A weave in which wefts are battened so closely together that they conceal warps.

TEMPER The addition of fine sand, powdered rock, or pulverized shards to clay to prevent a pot from cracking.

VEGETAL DYES Colors obtained from plants that grow on the reservation.

WARP The yarn stretched on a loom preparatory to weaving a tapestry. In basketry, warp is the stationary element or foundation.

WEFT The yarn woven over and under warps and from side to side in tapestry weaving. In basketry, weft is the element that is wrapped, woven, or stitched.

YARN, HANDSPUN Wool that has been hand cleaned, carded, and spun.

YARN, PROCESSED OR COMMERCIAL Commercially cleaned, carded, graded, and spun single-ply yarn.

YEI-BI-CHAI DANCE *See* Night Chant.

YEIS Important supernatural beings, also called the Holy People.

SUGGESTED READING

▼▼▼

Adair, John. *The Navajo and Pueblo Silversmiths.* University of Oklahoma Press. Norman, Oklahoma. 1944.

Alpert, Joyce M. "Kokopelli." *American Indian Art Magazine.* Scottsdale, Arizona. Winter 1991.

Anderson, Susanne. *Song of the Earth Spirit.* Friends of the Earth, Inc. New York. 1973.

Bennett, Edna Mae and John F. *Turquoise Jewelry of the Indians of the Southwest.* Turquoise Books. Colorado Springs, Colorado. 1973.

Berlant, Anthony and Mary Hunt Kahlenbert. "Walk in Beauty: The Navajo and Their Blankets." *American Indian Art Magazine.* Scottsdale, Arizona. Winter 1977.

Bialac, James T. "Drawn From Memory: The James T. Bialac Collection of Native American Art." The Heard Museum. Phoenix, Arizona. 1994–1995.

Bowers Museum. *Indian Basketry of Western North America.* Brooke House Publishers. Chatsworth, California. 1977.

Brugge, David M. *Hubbell Trading Post National Historic Site.* Southwest Parks and Monuments Association. Tucson, Arizona. 1993.

Brugge, David, Diane M. Wright, and Jan Bell. "Navajo Pottery." *Plateau* magazine. Museum of Northern Arizona. Flagstaff, Arizona. 1987.

Bulow, Ernie. *Navajo Taboos.* E. Bulow & Buffalo Medicine Books. Gallup, New Mexico. 1991.

Cerny, Charlene. *Navajo Pictorial Weaving.* The Museum of New Mexico Foundation. Santa Fe, New Mexico. 1975.

Chase, Katherine. "Navajo Painting." *Plateau* magazine. Museum of Northern Arizona. Flagstaff, Arizona. 1982.

Cirillo, Dexter. *Southwestern Indian Jewelry.* Abbeville Press. New York. 1992.

Dedera, Don. *Navajo Rugs: How to Find, Evaluate, Buy and Care for Them.* Northland Press. Flagstaff, Arizona. 1975.

De Lauer, Marjel. "Charles Loloma." *Arizona Highways.* Phoenix, Arizona. August 1976.

Dockstader, Frederick J. *Indian Art in North America.* New York Graphic Society. Greenwich, Connecticut. 1961.

Donovan, Bill. "Navajos Face Shortage of Medicine Men." *Indian Trader Newspaper.* Gallup, New Mexico. December 1991.

Dunn, Dorothy. *American Indian Painting of the Southwest and Plains Area.* University of New Mexico Press. Albuquerque, New Mexico. 1968.

Eaton, Linda B., Ph.D. *Native American Art of the Southwest.* Publications International, Ltd. Lincolnwood, Illinois. 1993.

Feder, Norman. *American Indian Art.* Harry N. Abrams, Inc. New York, New York. 1965.

Fergusson, Erna. *Dancing Gods.* University of New Mexico Press. Albuquerque, New Mexico. 1931.

Frank, Larry and Millard J. Holbrook, II. *Indian Silver Jewelry of the Southwest.* Schiffer Publishing, Ltd. West Chester, Pennsylvania. 1990.

Furst, Peter T. and Jill L. *North American Indian Art.* Rizzoli International Publications, Inc. New York. 1982.

Gilpin, Laura. *The Enduring Navaho.* University of Texas Press. Austin, Texas and London. 1968.

Gorman, R. C. "R. C. Gorman Speaks." *Indian Trader Newspaper.* Gallup, New Mexico. November 1993.

Griffin-Pierce, Trudy. "Navajo Ceremonial Sandpainting: Sacred, Living Entities." *American Indian Art Magazine.* Scottsdale, Arizona. Winter 1991.

Hartman, Russell and Jan Musial. *Navajo Pottery: Traditions & Innovations.* Northland Press. Flagstaff, Arizona. 1987.

Hedlund, Ann Lane. "Contemporary Navajo Weaving: Thoughts That Count." *Plateau* magazine. Museum of Northern Arizona. Flagstaff, Arizona. 1994.

Herold, Joyce. "Basket Weavers: Individualists in the Southwest Today." *American Indian Art Magazine.* Scottsdale, Arizona. Spring 1984.

Hill, Richard W., Sr. "The Battle Over Tradition." *Indian Artists Magazine.* Nightingale Hice, Inc. Santa Fe, New Mexico. Spring 1995.

James, H. L. *Posts and Rugs.* Southwest Parks and Monuments Association. Globe, Arizona. 1976.

Joe, Eugene Baatsoslanii, and Mark Bahti. *Navajo Sandpainting Art.* Walsworth Publishing Company. Marceline, Missouri. 1978.

Kaufman, Alice, and Christopher Selser. *The Navajo Weaving Tradition.* E. P. Dutton, Inc. New York. 1985.

Kawano, Kenji. *Warriors: Navajo Code Talkers.* Northland Publishing Company. Flagstaff, Arizona. 1990.

Kent, Kate Peck. *The Story of Navaho Weaving.* Heard Museum of Anthropology and Primitive Arts. Phoenix, Arizona. 1961.

Lester, Patrick. *The Biographical Directory of Native American Painters.* SIR Publications. Tulsa, Oklahoma. 1995.

Linford, Laurance D. *A Measure of Excellence.* Inter-Tribal Indian Ceremonial Association. Gallup, New Mexico. 1991.

Link, Martin A. *Navajo: A Century of Progress—1868–1968.* K. C. Publications. Flagstaff, Arizona. 1968.

Link, Martin A. *The Navajo Treaty— 1868.* K. C. Publications, Flagstaff, Arizona. 1988.

Manley, Ray. *Ray Manley's Collecting Southwestern Indian Arts & Crafts.* Ray Manley Publishing, Inc. Tucson, Arizona. 1979.

Manley, Ray, and Steve Getzwiller. *Ray Manley's The Fine Art of Navajo Weaving.* Ray Manley Publications. Tucson, Arizona. 1984.

Mason, Otis Tufton. *Aboriginal Indian Basketry.* The Rio Grande Press. Glorieta, New Mexico. 1902.

Maxwell, Gilbert S. *Navajo Rugs: Past, Present & Future.* Southwest Images. Santa Fe, New Mexico. 1963.

McCoy, Ronald. "The Healing Art of Sandpainting." *Indian Trader Newspaper.* Gallup, New Mexico. March 1989.

———. "Summoning the Gods: Sandpainting in the Native American Southwest." *Plateau* magazine.

Museum of Northern Arizona. Flagstaff, Arizona. 1988.

McCreevy, Susan Brown. "What Makes Sally Weave? Survival and Innovation in Navajo Basketry Trays." *American Indian Art Magazine.* Scottsdale, Arizona. Summer 1989.

———. "The Image Weavers: Contemporary Navajo Pictorial Textiles." *American Indian Art Magazine.* Scottsdale, Arizona. Autumn 1994.

Mercurio, Gian, and Maxymilian L. Peschel. *The Guide to Trading Posts and Pueblos.* Lonewolf Publishing. Cortez, Colorado. 1994.

Monthan, Guy and Doris. *Art and Indian Individualists.* Northland Press, Flagstaff, Arizona. 1975.

———. "Ha-So-De: One of the First Individualists," *American Indian Art Magazine.* Scottsdale, Arizona. Summer 1976.

Moore, Ellen K. "Designing with Light: Navajo Beadwork Today." *American Indian Art Magazine.* Scottsdale, Arizona. Autumn 1995.

Newman, Sandra Corrie. *Indian Basket Weaving.* Northland Press. Flagstaff, Arizona. 1974.

Reichard, Gladys A. *Navajo Medicine Man Sandpaintings.* Dover Publications, Inc. New York. 1977.

Snodgrass, Jeanne O. *Paintings from American Indian Painters: A Biographical Directory.* Museum of the American Indian Heye Foundation. New York. 1968.

Tanner, Clara Lee. *Indian Baskets of the Southwest.* University of Arizona Press. Tucson, Arizona. 1983

———. *Southwest Indian Craft Arts.* University of Arizona Press. Tucson, Arizona. 1968.

———. *Southwest Indian Painting.* University of Arizona Press. Tucson, Arizona. 1973.

Tanner, Rick. *The American Indians of Abeita: "His People."* Rick Tanner Publications. Scottsdale, Arizona. 1976.

Tryk, Sheila. *Santa Fe Indian Market.* Tierra Publications. Santa Fe, New Mexico. 1993.

Turnbaugh, William A. and Sarah Peabody Turnbaugh. *Indian Jewelry of the American Southwest.* Schiffer Publishing, Ltd. West Chester, Pennsylvania. 1988.

Tyner, Barbara. "Navajo Sandpaintings Are Going Upscale." *Indian Trader Newspaper.* Gallup, New Mexico. April 1993.

Villaseñor, David. *Tapestries in Sand: The Spirit of Indian Sandpainting.* Naturegraph Company. Healdsburg, California. 1963.

Wheat, Joe Ben. "The Navajo Chief Blanket." *American Indian Art Magazine.* Scottsdale, Arizona. Summer 1976.

Witherspoon, Gary. "Tension and Harmony: The Navajo Rug." *Plateau* magazine. Museum of Northern Arizona. Flagstaff, Arizona. 1981.

INDEX OF ARTISTS

▼▼▼

Abeita, Jim (Jimmie), 68, 78
Abeyta, Elizabeth, 93–94, 103
Abeyta, Narciso. *See* Ha-So-De
Abeyta, Tony, 67, 68–69, 83
Adaki, Jack, iv
Anderson, Evelyn, 11
Aragon, Joe, 97
Arviso, Julian, 10, 11
Ashley, Bah Yazzie, 96
Ashley, Leon, 11

Bahe, Bernice, 62
Barlow, Zonnie, iv
Begay, Calvin, 10, 14
Begay, Charlotte, 55
Begay, Elizabeth, 101
Begay, Harrison, 69, 71, 72, 75
Begay, J. M., 35
Begay, Jeanne, 39
Begay, Lorinda T., iv
Begay, Nina, 55
Begay, Sarah, 55
Begay, Sarah Paul, 44, 45
Begay, Stanley, 34, 39
Begay, Tony, 69–70, 73
Begay, Wanda, 39
Begaye, Nathan, 22
Ben, Mary L., 98
Ben, Rosabelle, 61
Benally, Johnny, Sr., 62
Benally, Kee Joe, iv, 16, 17
Benally, Kescoli the First, 97, 98
Bennett, Kay, 91, 101
Betoney, Betty, 10, 13
Betoney, Billy, 10, 13
Betsie, Maggie, 11
Beyale, Randall, 93, 102
Bia, Bessie, 48
Bia, Louise, 55
Bia, Susie, 101
Bicenti, Bessie, 37
Billie, Betty Rose, 10, 11
Billie, Rena, 55
Blackhat, Jean, 40, 43
Bluehorse, Leanne, 100

Brown, Durwin, 55
Brown, Lula, 55
Bryant, Kathy, 89

Cambridge, James M., 57
Cambridge, Samuel, 64
Castillo, Jeffrey, 99
Clark, David, 11
Claw, Bertha, 22
Claw, Silas, 8, 22, 24
Cling, Alice Williams, iv, 22, 27
Coan, Herman, 10
Cody, James, 70, 81
Conn, Minnie, iv
Crank, Susie, 27
Crosby, Brenda, 46
Curtis, Thomas, 99

Dempsey, A., 97
Desching, Isabelle, 38
Dougi, Tomas, Jr., 93, 101
Draper, Robert, 70, 79

Emerson, Nelson, 99
Endichy, Nora, 89

Franklin, W. B. (Bill), 70, 78
Fuller, Betty, 89
Fuller, Corena, iv, 89

Gaddy, Cora, 39
Geneeha, Garry, 92, 102
Gleason, Marie, 100
Goodman, Stella, 26
Gorman, R. C., 70, 75, 76

Ha-So-De, 68, 74, 93
Harrison, Nonabah, 41
Harvey, Jessie, 41
Henderson, Ella, iv
Henry, George, 17
Henry, Nuesie, 17
Holiday, Bessie, 97
Holiday family, iv
Hood, Tony, 70–71, 72, 74

Iskeets, Edison, 12

Jackson, Dan, 25
Jackson, Eugene, 11
Jackson, Tommy, iv, 10, 12
Jake, A., 7
James, Della, 10
James, Francis, 10
Jim, Anna Mae, 98
Joe, Daisy, iv
Joe, Eugene Baatsoslanii, 59, 64
Joe, Eunice, 42
Joe, James, 34, 42
Joe, Marie, 98
Joe, Marietta, iv
Joe, Shirley, 41
Johnson, Bobby, 60, 61
Judge, Raymond, 71, 79

Kahn, Chester, 15, 17
Kanuho, Sadie, 97
King, James, 71, 81

Lee, Allison, 13
Lee, Jerry, 71, 80
Lee, Tony, 64
Livingston, Jake, 92, 96, 100

Maloney, Louise, 48
Many Mules, Samuel, 25
Manygoats, Betty, 22, 26
Mark, Lorraine, 55
Martin, Helen, 55
Martinez, Calvin, iv
McCabe, Louise, 25
McHorse, Christine, iv, 22
McKelvey, Cecilia, 23
McKelvey, Celeste, 23
McKelvey, Celinda, 23
McKelvey, Lucy Leuppe, 19, 22–23
Monongye, Jesse, 10, 14
Monroe, Jean, 52
Morgan, Elsie K., 100
Morris, Shilene, 91, 98
Mountain, Rena, 43, 52

Murphy, Benjamin, 11
Muskett, Wilbert, Jr., 10, 14

Nells, Jerry, 64
Nelson, Doreen, 25
Nelson, Emmett, 13
Nelson, Howard, 14
Nelson, Roger, 25
Nez, Felicia, 98
Nez, Gibson, 10, 12
Nez, Leslie, 92, 94
Nez, Marjorie, iv
Nez, Mary C., 38
Nez, Nadine, 55
Nez, Redwing T., 71, 77
Nez, Rose Marie, 55

Owens, Rose, 31, 51
Owl, Bessie, 97

Perez, Alverez, 13
Platero, Alice, iv

Roan, Marilyn, 39
Roanhorse, 98
Roanhorse, Elizabeth, 39
Roanhorse, Lucy, 55
Ross, Sadie, 46, 51
Rotsinah, Wilford, 64
Rotsinah, Wilfred, iv

Sahmie, Ida, 22, 44
SAW, 27
Scott, Willie, 44
Secody, Mary, 89
Sellers, Bessie, 52
Shepard, Mary, 41
Shirley, Ed, 10
Silversmith, Deborah, 12
Slick, Jennie, 85
Sloan, Mary, 51
Smith, Henry Lee, 12
Spencer, Charley, 99
Spencer, Lorenzo, 26

Tabaha, Francis, 14
Tahoma, Quincy, 71, 76
Taylor, Robert, 14
Thomas, Diane, 63
Tisi, Sarah, 55
Toddy, Calvin, 71, 72, 76
Toddy, Irving, 71–72, 77, 80
Toddy, Jimmy, Sr. *See* Yazz, Beatien
Tolino, Rick, 14
Tracey, Ray, 10, 17
Tsinnie, Janet, iv
Tsinnie, Jolene, 98
Tsinnie, Orville, 25
Tsinnie, Shirley, 96
Tsinnijinnie, Mary, 38
Tso, Emmett, 22
Tso, Faye, 22, 26
Tso, Myra, 26
Tso, Sarah, 49
Tso, Tina, 26
Tsosie, Boyd, 10, 15
Tsosie, Mike, 96
Tsosie, Nellie, 101
Tsosie, Nora, iv
Tsosie, Wilson, 10

Van Winkle, Lorene, 38

Wadsworth, Mary, 54
Warren, Lillie, 41
Washburn, Tim, 92–93, 102
Watchman, Alfred, 60
Watchman, Bruce, 72, 74
Waters, Rachael, iv
White, Ruby, 47
Whitney, Cara, 37, 38
Williams, Lorraine, iv, 25, 26
Wilson, Lucy, 49

Yazz, Beatien, 71–72, 73
Yazzie, Albert, 63
Yazzie, Annie, 41
Yazzie, Bessie, 98
Yazzie, Darlene, 55

Yazzie, Fannie, iv
Yazzie, Gloria, 35, 41
Yazzie, Joe D., iv
Yazzie, Larry, 93, 103
Yazzie, Lee, 10, 17
Yazzie, Mary Marie, 16
Yazzie, Matilda, 55
Yazzie, Minnie, 55
Yazzie, Nellie, 55
Yazzie, Raymond, 17
Yazzie, Tom W., 72, 74, 92, 95
Yellowhair, Laura, 100
Yellowhair, Rosie, 62
Yellowhorse, Dererie, 12

GENERAL INDEX

▼▼▼

Abalone Woman, 1
Abeyta, Sylvia Ann, 93
After the Rain, 103
Alabaster, 92–93, *101, 102*
American Indian Arts School, 92
American Indian Movement, 69
Apaches, 86
Art Institute of Chicago, 68
Awaiting a Storm, 79

Baskets, *84,* 85–88, *89, 97, 98*
    caring for, 88
    ceremonial, 86
    mountain mahogany in, 86
    new motifs, 88
    pitch coating, 85–86, *97*
    spirit line, 87
    sumac in, 86–87
    and taboos, 86, 88
    utilitarian, 86
    water jar, 85
    wedding, *i, iv, 56, 84,* 85, 86,
        87–88, *89, 98*
Basketweavers, 88
Bayeta, 32
Beadwork, 91, *100*
Belt, *98.* See also Belt buckles,
    Concha belts
Belt buckles, *12, 13, 14, 16, 17. See also*
    Concha belts
Beyond Native Tradition, 45
Beyond Navajo Tradition, 44
Biss, Earl, 68
Black Dancers, 5
Blankets. *See* Chief Blankets, Saddle
    blankets, Wearing blankets
The Blessing of Shiprock, 81
Bola ties, *i,* iv, *6, 7, 17*
Bosque Redondo, 2, 7
Bracelets, *i, iv, viii, 6, 7, 10, 11, 12,*
    14, 17
Bureau of Indian Affairs, 71
Burnham, Bruce, 30, 33

Burnham, Virginia, 97
Burntwater rugs, 29, *37, 38, 45*
Butterfly Maiden Kachina, 17
Buttons, *98, 100*

Carson, Kit, 2
Ceramic mask, 97
Chair, *97*
Chants, 4, 57–58
Chicken Pull, 68, *74*
Chief Blankets, 32, *41, 42*
    phases, 32, *41, 42*
Child-Born-of-the-Water, 74
Cloth dolls, *90,* 91, *98, 101*
Coal Mine Mesa, 30
Code Talkers, 3–4
Concha belts, *i,* iv, *viii,* 8, *13, 16, 17.*
    See also Belt, Belt buckles
Coral, 8, *12, 16*
Corn Yeis, *47*
Cradleboards, 92, *97*
Crystal rugs, 30, 33
Currency Defacement Act, 8

Diné, 1. *See also* Navajo
Dontso figures, *37*
"The Dream," 44
The Dreamer, 80
Dress, *98*
Dunn, Dorothy, 67–68, 69, 70
Dusk, 76

Earrings, *14*
Earth People, 1
Enemy Way, 5
Entah. *See* Enemy Way
Evening Herd, 77
Evening Stroll, 77

Feather Maiden, 59, *62*
Fifteen-in-One rugs, 31, *55*
First Man, 87
First Woman, 87

Flute Players, *14*
Fort Defiance, 2
Fort Sumner, 2, 8
Four Sacred Plants, 59
Four-in-One rugs, 31, *43*
Fourth World, 87
Fox Tail Dancers Rugs, *48*
Fred Harvey Company, 32
Friends of Lorenzo Hubbell, 3
Fringe Mouth, *74*
Furniture, *97*

Gallup Inter-Tribal Indian Ceremonial,
    14, 33, 38, 60, 71
Ganado rugs, 29, 30, 31, *41, 96*
Germantown rugs, 31, 40
Glittering World, 87
Gods of Harvest, *62*
Gold, 10, *11, 14*

Hannum, Alberta, 72
Holy People, 1, 31, 59
Hopi, 5, 8, 30, 56, 59
Houser, Allan, 68
How To Do Permanent Sandpainting, 58
How-To-Do-Sandpainting Kit, 58
Hózhó, 1, 57
Hubbell, John Lorenzo, 3, 8–9, 32, 33
Hubbell Trading Post, 3, 8, 33
Hump-backed Yeis, *47*
    sandpaintings, 59
The Hunters, 79
Hyde Exploring Expedition, 32

Indian Art School, 72
Institute of American Indian Art, 68, 93
Invocation, 103

Jet Black Woman, 1
Jewelry, 6–17
    age and value, 9
    materials, 9–10
    social and economic functions, 9

Judge, Rose, 71
Judge, Slim, 71

Keam, Thomas, 33
Ketohs, *6, 7, 8, 14*
Kinaaldá, 88, 91, *101*
Kirsten, 75
Klagetoh rugs, 30, *41*
Klah, Hosteen, 30

Lapis lazuli, *12*
Like Father Like Son: Gourd Dancers, 102
Link, Martin, 3
Lippincott, Bill, 72
Lippincott, Sallie, 72
Little Summer Thunders, *62, 64*
Long Walk, 2
The Long Walk, 70
Looms, 31, *43*

Malone, Bill, 3, 33
Man with Bola Tie and Earring, 78
Marble, 93
Maryland Institute of Fine Arts, 68
Medicine men, 4, 47, 57, 58, 87
    restrictions on pottery, 19–20
Memory, 101
Mexico City College, 70
A Midnight Prayer, 101
Midnight Whistle, 78
Montoya, Gerónima Cruz, 68
Moonlit Night, 81
Moore, J. B., 29, 33
Mormon Church, 92
Mother and Child, 73
Mother Earth and Father Sky, 46
*Mother Earth, Father Sky Contemplating
the Science of Spirituality, 83*
Mountain mahogany, 86
Mt. Blanca, Colorado, 1
Mt. Hesperus, Colorado, 1
Mt. Taylor, New Mexico, 1
Mud Dance, 5

Mud Head Clowns, *103*
Museum of Northern Arizona Navajo
    Show, 25, 41, 103
"My Precious Child," 45

Naf-bah, 100
Naja, 8
Namingha, Dan, 68
Native American Church, 5, 92
Navajo
    arrival in Southwest, 2
    and art, 67
    chants, 4, 57–58
    Christians among, 5
    Code Talkers, 3–4
    and Hopi, 5, 30
    housing, 3
    kinship with Athapascan tribes, 2
    Long Walk, 2
    medicine men, 4
    and Mexicans, 5
    natural resources, 1–2
    occupations, 3
    and painting, 67
    population, 2
    silversmithing, 5, 7–9, *95*
    territory, *4*
    tribal government, 2
    and trucks, 3
    weaving, 5
    young people, 4
    and Zuni, 5
Navajo Community College, 4, 93
Navajo Nation, 1–2
    map, *4*
Navajo Nation Museum, 92
Necklaces, *12, 14, 16, 17, 25, 56*
    squash blossom, *i,* iv, *vii,* 8, *10, 14,
        17, 98, 100*
New Lands rugs, 30
New Mexico State Fair, 71, 95
Night Chant. *See* Yei-bi-chai Dance
Night Dance, 87

Night Way. *See* Yei-bi-chai Dance

O'odham Tash Show, 97
Orozco, 70

Paint the Wind, 72
Painters, 68–72
Painting, 67–68
    easel, 67–68
    in Navajo society, 67
Paintings, *66, 73–83*
Paiutes, 86, 87
Peace Offering, 102
Pendants, iv, *viii, 6, 7*
Peter, James, 23
Peyote Sacrament, 5
Pictorial rugs, 30–31, *49, 51, 52*
Pins, *35, 98*
Pots, i, iv, *viii, 18,* 19, *24–27, 44, 56*
    drum pots, 22
Potters, 22–23
Pottery, 19–23
    appliqué, 21
    carving, 21–22
    ceremonial use, 19, 20
    coil-and-scrape method, 20
    current revival, 20, 23
    decline of tradition with arrival of
        trading posts, 19
    drum pots, 22
    drying, 20
    family participation, 22
    finishing and decorating techniques,
        21–22
    fire clouds, 21
    firing, 20–21
    forms, 22
    incising, 21
    modeling, 21
    ping test, 21
    pinyon pitch finish, 21
    potters, 22–23
    preparing clay, 20

and Pueblo pottery, 20, 22
restrictions by medicine men and
  traditionalists, 19–20
Shonto-Cow Springs area, 20, 22
spirit line, 21
stamping, 21

Rainbow God, *37, 46*
Rainbow Goddess, *60*
R. B. Burnham Trading Post, 33
Remembrance of a Past Love Song, 101
Rings, *6, 7, 10, 14, 15*
Rio Grande Waterfowl, 82, 83
Rivera, 70
Round rugs, 31, *51*
Royal Web Gemstone, 17
Rugs, *28,* 29–34, *34–55,* 98
  assessing, 33–34
  Burntwater, iv, *vi,* 29, *37, 38, 45*
  care of, 34
  Chief Blankets, 32, *41, 42*
  Crystal, 30, 33
  Fifteen-in-One, 31, *55*
  Four-in-One, 31, *43*
  Fox Tail Dancers, *48*
  Ganado, 29, 30, 31, *41, 96*
  Germantown, 31, *40*
  Klagetoh, 30, *41*
  looms, 31, *43*
  miniature, *55, 101*
  New Lands, 30
  Pictorial, 30–31, *49, 51, 52*
  Round, 31, *51*
  saddle blankets, 31, *34*
  Sandpainting, 30, 46
  Sawmill, 31, 41
  Spider Woman, *50,* 51
  spirit line, 31
  Storm Pattern, *i, iv,* 31, *43*
  Teec Nos Pos, iv, *vi,* 29–30, *41*
  Teec Nos Pos Eyedazzler, 31, *35*
  Thirty-in-One, 31, *44*
  transition replica, iv, *viii*

Tree of Life, 30–31, *36,* 52, *52, 53*
Twenty-Four-in-One, 31, *45,* 52, *53*
Two Grey Hills, 29, 33, 44, *44, 54,* 98
Two-Faced, 31, *49*
vegetal dyes, 30, *38, 39*
wearing blankets, 32, *35*
Whirling Logs, *46*
Wide Ruins, 30, *38, 39, 45*
Yei, 31, *47*
Yei-bi-chai, 31, *48, 49*

Sacred Circle, 80
Sacred mountains, 1
Saddle blankets, 31, *34, 96, 98*
Saddle Throw, *35*
Saddlebags, *96*
Saddles and saddle making, 92, *96*
Salako Kachina, *57*
San Francisco Art Institute, 93
San Francisco Peaks, 1
Sandpainting rugs, 30, 46
Sandpaintings, *i,* iv, *56,* 57–60, *60–65.*
  See also Sandpainting rugs
  ceremonial, 57–58
  creating sand, 59
  criticism of, 59
  and healing, 58
  Hopi Kachina Dancers, *63*
  Hump-backed Yeis, 59, *62*
  with oil or acrylic, 60, *61*
  outlining in glue, 59
  permanent, 58–59
  purchasing guidelines, 60
  shellac coating, 59
  Storm Pattern, 59
  technique, 59
  Whirling Logs, 59, *60, 63*
  Yei-bi-chai, 59
  Yei figures, *61*
Sani, Atsidi, 7
Santa Fe Indian Market, 33, 71
Santa Fe Indian School, 67, 69, 70
Sawmill rugs, 31, 41

Scholder, Fritz, 68
Scott, Preston, 78
Sculpture, 92–93, *95, 100–103*
Shonto-Cow Springs area, 20, 22
Silver, *6,* 7, *10–17, 99*
Silversmithing, 5, 7–9, *95*
Siqueros, 70
Smallcanyon, Ceclone, 93
Snake Yeis, *47*
Spider Woman rug, *50,* 51
Spin a Silver Dollar, 72
Spirit line
  baskets, 87
  pottery, 21
  rugs, 31
Squash blossom necklaces, *i, iv, viii,* 8,
  10, 15, 17, 98, *100*
Squaw Dance, 5. *See also* Enemy Way
Steatite, 93
Storm Pattern
  rugs, 31, *43*
  sandpaintings, 59
String ties, *13*
The Studio, 68
Sumac, 86–87

Talking God, 74
Tanglechee, Daisy, 29
Teec Nos Pos Eyedazzler rugs, 31, *35*
Teec Nos Pos rugs, iv, *vi,* 29–30, *41*
Tending the Flock, 75
Thirty-in-One rugs, 31, *44*
Ties, *13. See also* Bola ties, String ties
Tobacco canteen, *i,* iv
Today's Journey, 76
Toddy, Frances, 72
Toddy, Jimmy Jr., 72
Toddy, Marvin, 72
Toddy, Orland, 72
Torch to Start the Squaw Dance, 69, *75*
Traders, 2–3
Tree of Life rugs, 30–31, *36,* 52, *52, 53*
Tufa, *10*

Turquoise, *6*, 7, 8–9, *10, 11, 13, 15, 17, 98, 100*
  importance of, 9
  sources, 9
Turquoise Woman, 1
Twenty-Four-in-One rugs, 31, *45*, 52, *53*
Two-Faced rugs, 31, *49*
Two Grey Hills rugs, 29, 33, 44, *44, 54, 98*

Utes, 86

Vases
  wedding, iv, *viii*
Vegetal dyes, 30, *38, 39*
Villaseñor, David, 58
Villaseñor, Jean, 58

War Ceremony, 5
Watch tips, *13*
Wearing blankets, 32, *35*
The Weaver, 73
Weavers Image, 78
Weaving, 31–34
  assessing, 33–34
  beginnings, 31–32
  Classic Period, 32
  economic aspects, 32–33
  future of, 34
  looms, 31, *43*
  Revival Period, 32–33
  Rug Period, 32
  Transition Period, 32
  vegetal dyes, 30, *38, 39*
  wool, 32, 33
Wedding baskets, *i*, iv, *56, 84,* 85, 86, 87–88, *89, 98*
Wetherill, Richard, 33
Whirling Logs
  rug, *46*
  sandpaintings, 59, *60, 63*
White Shell Woman, 1
Wide Ruins rugs, 30, *38, 39, 45*

Windway Medicine Man, 23
Wintering Below Chuska Mountain, 76
Wood carving, *44,* 72, *74,* 92, *94*

Yei-bi-chai Dance, 4–5, *44, 44*
Yei-bi-chai figures, 22, 23, *44,* 66, 67, *97*
Yei-bi-chai rugs, 31, *48, 49*
  sandpaintings, 59
Yei figures, *i*, iv, 23, *46*
  sandpaintings, *61*
Yei rugs, 31, *47*
Yeis
  Corn, *47*
  Hump–backed, *47*
  Snake, *47*
Zuni, 5, 8, 56

ABOUT THE AUTHOR

THEDA BASSMAN was led by back-packing and river-running exploits into Arizona and New Mexico, where she was pleased to find that her feelings for nature and the environment were rather similar to those expressed by many Native Americans of the region. She developed many friendships within the Native American communities in a short period of time. For the past fifty years she has traveled to the Indian reservations, not only to visit her friends but to buy their crafts. In 1972 she opened a gallery in Beverly Hills, California, called The Indian and I. When she and her husband retired, they moved to Palm Desert, California, where they now live. They also have a cabin on the Mogollon Rim in northern Arizona, where they spend their time in the forest and traveling to the nearby Indian reservations. Theda has judged Indian Shows at the Museum of Northern Arizona in Flagstaff, Arizona; The Inter-Tribal Indian Ceremonial in Gallup, New Mexico; the Santa Fe Indian Market in Santa Fe, New Mexico; the O'Odham Tash in Casa Grande, Arizona; and the American Indian and Western Relic Show in Pasadena, California. Theda Bassman is a feminist, an environmentalist, and a lover of chamber music. She is a member of Greenpeace, the Sierra Club, and the Hemlock Society, and is a Hospice volunteer.

Chris Everett

ABOUT THE PHOTOGRAPHER

GENE BALZER is a professor of photography at Northern Arizona University in Flagstaff. He has photographed most of the collection of the Museum of Northern Arizona, also in Flagstaff, and conducts field trips to various archaeological sites and national parks on the Colorado Plateau. Balzer's photographs have appeared in *Arizona Highways, American Indian Art Magazine, Southwest Profile, Plateau* magazine, *The World and I,* and *The Indian Country Guide.* One of his photographs was featured on the cover of a compact disc by Native American flutist R. Carlos Nakai. Balzer is the photographer for all of Theda Bassman's books.